A MUNSEY-HOPKINS GENEALOGY

Being the Ancestry of

ANDREW CHAUNCEY MUNSEY

AND

MARY JANE MERRITT HOPKINS

The Parents of

FRANK A. MUNSEY

HIS BROTHER AND SISTERS

By D. O. S. LOWELL, A. M., M. D., Litt. D.

*Head Master of the Roxbury Latin School. Life Member of the
New England Historic-Genealogical Society.*

PRIVATELY PRINTED
BOSTON
1920

PREFACE

In the preparation of these Genealogical Lines, a great deal of original work has been done. Nothing had ever been published on the Munsey Line, and the solution of its connection with the various allied lines involved much travel and painstaking research. The carelessness with which original records were made; the loss or destruction of many, owing to Indian massacres, fires, indifference, or neglect,— all these drawbacks make the work of the genealogist fascinating, yet unspeakably difficult.

In the collection of the material needed for this little volume, the writer has been greatly aided by Mr. William Lincoln Palmer of Boston, himself a life member of the New England Historic-Genealogical Society and corresponding member of the New York Genealogical and Biographical Society, etc. His patience and genius have unravelled many a tangled skein; and before the burning of the City Hall building, at Portland, Maine, and the State Library at Albany, N. Y., he copied records that now exist only in these pages.

Great care has been taken to verify all statements that are not shown to be unproved. If there be errors in the work, they have crept in, in spite of continual watchfulness.

The Ancestral Chart, which shows at a glance the lines of descent described in the text, has been prepared especially for this work by Mr. J. Gardner. Bartlett; a constant reference to this will serve greatly to aid the reader.

From the nature of the case, the authorities proving the Munsey Line consist mainly of a wealth of MSS. in the writer's possession, compiled from deeds, wills, affidavits, and attested copies of town, county, state, and national records. The authorities for the Hopkins Line and the other allied families are given at the close of each genealogy.

Boston, January, 1920.

D. O. S. Lowell.

CONTENTS

(The names in red in this table denote maternal ancestors of Frank A. Munsey)

INTRODUCTION

THE REASON FOR THIS GENEALOGY

It was a tradition with my grandfather Hopkins that his family was directly descended from Stephen Hopkins of the *Mayflower*. Whether he had any real interest in the tradition or not, I do not know. It would have been out of the usual if he had, since the people of his generation and the generations that preceded him in New England of early American stock, particularly those in the farming communities, had few, if any, authentic family records running further back than a grandfather or great-grandfather. Even these shorter ancestral spans were not always trustworthy. Usually they were mere memories, not written documents, and mere memories are not likely to be any too authentic in the matter of history, human or otherwise.

The people of my grandfather's period, however, were neither worse nor better than their early colonial ancestors. Indeed, the absence of trustworthy family records all the way down from the time of the Pilgrim settlers was so well nigh universal throughout New England, that it would almost seem that all interest in ancestry was regarded as a kind of snobbishness unbecoming in the hard working, God-fearing American—unbecoming, unmanly, or even sinful.

For aught I know, my grandfather may have had a keen desire to know something of his ancestors beyond the mere tradition that Stephen Hopkins was one of them—to know something definite and positive. But however keen the desire may have been in his heart, what could he do about it? There were no genealogical libraries at his command, and in fact in his day comparatively few New Englanders had taken the trouble to trace back their ancestors and to have the record published.

It required money then, as now, to dig out these family facts, and my grandfather, though a "comfortably off" farmer, had little to spare for anything save the necessities and "reasonable comforts" incident to life on a Maine farm,—when a Maine farm was largely surrounded by wilderness and the absence of neighbors, and was notably lacking in the present-day niceties of living.

However my grandfather may have viewed the question of ancestry, it is certain that his daughter, my mother, had a keen interest in the Hopkins family tradition that linked her in blood and character through the long past with that wonderful *Mayflower* band of pioneers. My mother's soul craved all that was best in life. God gave her imagination and ambition—not a frivolous ambition, but the kind that rang true to her Puritan ancestry—the ambition that made New England the dominating and leavening force of all America and the inspiration of the world. God gave her, too, a strong religious nature, and the instincts and character of the true woman, qualities that made her the devoted, loyal, and helpful wife and the loving, thoughtful mother, able, resourceful, an inspiration to husband and children alike; self-sacrificing, patient, sunny. Such was my mother.

One of my mother's unsatisfied desires was to know—actually to know—whether the old Hopkins family tradition was really true. Her faith, buttressed by the scraps of information she had gathered from here and there, told her that it was true, but at best a genealogical tradition is not very satisfying. Nothing short of documentary evidence is satisfying to one who cares for accuracy and honesty.

The greatest regret of my life, since my income began to mount, has been that my mother was not with me to make free use of it. It would have enabled her to do the things and have the things that her fine, true nature craved. With Saint Paul, she could then have said truly, that "faith is the substance of things hoped for, the evidence of things not seen." The dreams of ambition, in so far as concerns the opening up of the big world to her and to her family, would have come true. I know with deep appreciation what these dreams and aspirations must have been, for I am her son.

Beyond so living and achieving as to reflect honor on one's parents,—so living and achieving as to meet in reasonable measure their ambitions and ideals for a son,—there is little else one can do for them when death has gathered them to its fold. There are some small services, like carrying out their wishes with respect to persons and things,—some undertakings that they themselves would have put through, given time and means and opportunity,— that a son may put through for them. One of these services, with me, was to do for my mother what she would have liked to do for herself with respect to the *Mayflower* ancestry of her family. It was the thought of doing this little thing for her that prompted me to have the Hopkins genealogy worked out, or rather so much of it as would make clear the truth or falsity of the Hopkins family tradition. I had no other purpose in the undertaking.

Unable to give to the subject the time it required, I commissioned my friend, Dr. D. O. S. Lowell of Boston, to do the work for me. It was not many months after he began his task when I found I was committed to the production of a regular family genealogy. It seems that a serious start at tracing any phase of family history always ends in this way.

Dr. Lowell had in fact worked out the skeleton of a general genealogy, covering both my father's and mother's families, before telling me that there was no place to stop, short of a fairly complete work. And in the search for the missing link in the Hopkins chain which he had not yet found, he had uncovered a veritable gold mine of *Mayflower* ancestry through my mother's mother's family, the Spragues. Moreover, he urged that having the means to carry on the research, I owed it to New England, as a contribution to the history of that section, to do so.

There was no ground for controverting his reasoning, and so the work went on. Its merits as a historical document bearing on many of the early New England settlers rest fully with Dr. Lowell. Its shortcomings or errors, if there be such, rest equally on him.

Personally I have contributed nothing to the

work, save in the method of handling the facts. To my mind a genealogy should not be a family biography, but rather a mirror of the many human strata that merge in an individual. Accordingly I asked Dr. Lowell to hold to this formula in compiling the record. It is certain that the completed book is less warm, has less color and less of personal interest than it would have had, had Dr. Lowell been free to follow his own preferences. I take the blame fully for this defect, if it be a defect *in a genealogy.*

As the work pertaining to this genealogy was undertaken because of my mother,—not my father,—it follows naturally that in the opening of this Introduction I had to confine myself to her and her family. But having said what I have of my mother, it follows naturally also that I must say something of my father, else he would seem so unimportant a member of the family as not to merit a word of tribute from me.

My mother in a womanly way had a well-defined and positive individuality; my father had a much stronger, more definite, more positive individuality. My mother was conventional in viewpoint and gracious in bearing; my father, while not ungracious, was rugged, clean-cut, and of the type that hews straight to the line. He was not a round-cornered man; he was distinctly a square-cornered man, who stood rigidly for square-cornered honesty and square-cornered uprightness. Nothing so annoyed him as pretense and hypocrisy. Half-way-right things were not right at all in his eyes. His was a critical, painstaking, analytical nature,— but withal a sympathetic, generous, tender nature.

He had in him little of the spirit of compromise. The best within his means was the only thing he would tolerate. It did not make him unhappy to go without the things he would have liked to have. He preferred this to any compromise with his well-defined taste. And in the matter of his friendships the same spirit ruled him, though he loved people and had essentially a social nature. Quality, alike in people and in things, appealed to him. This was equally true of my mother, but she could compromise, as women can, while my father could not.

In early life one accepts one's father and mother as just *father* and *mother;* that's all, and that's enough. They are something apart from other men and women. Their qualities of mind and heart are not analyzed or their abilities measured. I really never knew my father until I saw him in his last great battle. The issue was with Death. Though old in years, having to his credit eighty-six summers, he met it as he had met all other issues in life, with a will to conquer. I was then a mature man, as I watched for days by his bedside, seeing and feeling that the end was not far off. In these trying, watchful hours I went back over my father's life and came to see him as I had never before known him.

He came on the stage of young manhood when Maine was a semi-wilderness. There were few openings for advancement in the rural sections. Saving up money as capital with which to make a start in life was a slow business. How far my father had progressed in this respect when he married I do not know, but I do know that marriage put an end to it. From that time on it was always a question of making a good home for his wife and children. He could embark on no venture, could take no chances, and so he lived out his days and died without knowing—save for his own consciousness—the quality of the faculties he had in him. The story of his life as I saw it deepened the shadows, and the more so as the thought clung to me that his harder life—his failure to reap the harvest of his excellent abilities—had perhaps contributed in no small measure to my own life-work.

FRANK A. MUNSEY.

PART I

THE MUNSEY LINE

In PART I, names printed in LARGE CAPITALS
denote direct ancestors of Frank A. Munsey.

PART I

THE MUNSEY LINE

The Source of the Munsey Name

The name MUNSEY, though not common, seems to be very ancient. One eminent authority (Dr. Whitaker) maintains that it is of Roman origin. He says:

"If the Romans left us few Roman names of towns or cities, they have left us their own names, which their lineal descendants still bear, and which cannot on any intelligible principle be traced to another origin, Saxon, Danish, or Norman. No serious doubt can be entertained that the families Marsh, MOUNSEY [an English variant of MUNSEY], Tully, Rosse, Cecil, and Manley, derive their names and blood from the Roman families, viz., Martia, MONTIA, Tullia, Roscia, Caecilia, and Manlia. These, and many others, are descended from Roman legionaries."

Still we must not suppose that those names were left behind by the Roman legionaries in Britain. Most of them undoubtedly were brought to England from Normandy, and therefore if Dr. Whitaker is right (and his argument seems reasonable), they must have been reliques of the Roman legionaries in Gaul.

As regards the English name MUNSEY (MOUN-SEY), it is probably from the Norman or French "Monceaux." Those bearing the name may have descended from the Roman family Montia, whose places, or seats, named after them are numerous. These are found in old maps of France:

Monceau, on the river Saonne, in Burgundy.

Monceaux, near Sezanne, in Champagne.

Monceaux l'Abbaye, in Picardy, S. of Aumale.

Monceaux à Chiens, near Criquetot, in Normandy.

Monchy le Preux, near Senarpont, N. of Forest of Eu.

Monchy, S. of Eu in Normandy.

In Taylor's translation of Wace's Chronicle of the Dukes of Normandy, he supposes the seat of the De Monceaux, there referred to, to have been the Commune of Monceaux, in Boyeux, in the Bessin. But it seems more likely that the branch of the family which came with the Conqueror to England was from the Castle and Castellany of Monceaux, in the County of Eu. These are named in the Norman Rolls, A.D. 1418-19. After the Conquest an English De Monceaux is closely connected with the Earls of Eu in England, and had probably formed a part of the Earl of Eu's contingent in the Conqueror's army. Foxe, in his "Acts and Monuments", gives "the names of those that were at the conquest of England." One of the lines in this list runs:

"Le Sire de Monceaulx."

Copies purporting to have been made from the

original roll of Battle Abbey contain the same name under different forms: Mounchensey, Mountchensey, Monceus, Mouncey, Mouncy, and Monceals.

From these concurring statements we are led to believe that more than one Monceaux was with Duke William at Hastings. Of one of these we at once find traces in southern England. Robert, Earl of Eu or Au, received, as a reward for his services, the Rape of Hastings. Within that territory are Hurstmonceaux and Bodiham, both of which were subsequently held by the family of Monceaux under the Earls of On. To the former their name adhered and yet remains. In Domesday Book it is simply "Herste" in the tenure of the Earl of On, by whom no doubt it was granted in subinfeudation to his faithful follower De Monceaux, who made it his seat and stamped it with his name.

To this day the local pronunciation of *Hurstmonceaux* is "Harzmounsey" or "Harsmouncy*," a strong evidence of the identity of the ancient Norman Monceaux with the modern English MOUNSEY (MUNSEY).

In France the name, after various changes, seems to have crystallized into a form not unlike the English—Moncey. Thus one of Napoleon's marshals, described by Headley, was Bon-Adrien Moncey (1754–1842). Being a successful general, he was made a Marshal of France 19 May, 1804, and Duke of Conegliano in 1808.

Surnames were not in use in either England or

* *Notes and Queries*, Vol. V., page 499.

Scotland before the Norman Conquest, and are first to be found in the Domesday Book. It is stated on good authority that the most ancient surnames were derived from places in Normandy; that they were usually preceded by De, Du, De La, or Des, and began or ended with Mont, Beau, Ville, and the like. With these conditions, De Monceaus, De Monceaux, Monceaulx, Mountsey, and many other early forms comply; therefore the inference is reasonable that this name was originally at least Norman, if not Roman.

It was during the reign of Edward I that the English name De Monceaux began to assume its modern shape; and curiously enough the change seemingly arose not in England, but on the Continent. The stages through which it passed were something like the following: Mounceaux, Monceaux, Monceau, Mouncey, Mounsey, Munsey. From 1291 to 1300 we find a burgess of Berwick, on the Scottish border, and a Baron and Lord of Parliament, Walter de Mouncey (also spelled Mouncy, Moncy, and Monci), dwelling at the court of Edward I, and Chamberlain to the Prince who was afterwards King Edward II.

Of the various families of De Monceaux which entered England at the time of the Norman invasion, some settled in the south; some went to the north, especially to the counties of Cumberland and Westmoreland; others even crossed the Scottish border. Then they apparently began to gravitate toward London, settling in Cambridgeshire and other counties on the way. At the close of the sixteenth and the opening of the seventeenth centuries, several of this rare name were living in London itself. Finally, about the middle of the seventeenth century, a few of the more adventurous spirits made their way across the Atlantic.

THE APPEARANCE OF THE MUNSEY NAME IN AMERICA

The first record of the Munseys in America is found in Ipswich, Mass., where a Francis[1] Munsey married, in 1659, Hannah, daughter of William Adams. It is worthy of note that the first Munsey that has been found in America was himself a "Frank" Munsey. A son John[2] was born to Francis and his wife in 1660. About 1664 they removed to Brookhaven, Long Island, N. Y. There a second son, Samuel,[2] was born about 1675. Shortly after this, Francis[1] died. His son John[2] married Hannah Brewster, a great-granddaughter of Elder William Brewster, of *Mayflower* fame. John died at the age of 30, in 1690/91. In a nuncupative will he speaks of his brother Samuel[2] and a son John[3].

A Thomas[1] Munsey is found in New York City, in 1693±, as Surveyor of the Port; in 1697 we also find him as Deputy Collector.

It is WILLIAM[1] MUNSEY, however, who most interests us, since he is the earliest *known* ancestor of those with whose line we are especially concerned.

In the clerk's office at Patchogue, N. Y., there is mention of *a* William Munsey. The date is 1678,

or earlier. In the record of a drawing for 50 town
"lotts" we find the following list:

not william muncy	ould John
Mr. Wodhull	1 blank
Zachary Hawkins	1 blank
William Sallier	1 blank
Andrew Miller	2 blanks
Thomas Smith	1 blank
etc., etc.	

Evidently after "william muncy" had been written, the word "not" was inserted before "william";
then both words ("not william") were lined through
rather clumsily with a pen, and "ould John" was
written after "muncy."

What shall we infer from this?

First of all, that *there was a William Munsey* in the
mind of the scribe, and probably in the vicinity;
second, that he was *not* the man who drew for the lot;
and third, that "ould John" Somebody drew (a
blank, doubtless), and "not william muncy."

Then the question arises, Does "muncy ould
John" signify *Old John Munsey?* We can find no
trace of a John Munsey in America older than the
son of Francis[1], who was born in 1660, and therefore
was about eighteen at this time. We have seen that
he speaks of a son John[3] in 1690, the year of his death;
but even then—at the age of 30—it is not likely that
he would have been called "ould John." Elsewhere
in the Patchogue records an "old John Thompson"
is mentioned; so we suspect that he is the person
referred to, and that the line of erasure ought to run
through the "muncy" as well as through the "not

william." Either the scribe was careless or his successor reckless, for the next entry—"Mr. Wodhull" —has a cross upon the "d," which looks like an attempt to strike out that name, too.

It may well be that the William Munsey who did *not* draw a town lot at Patchogue in 1678 was the same one who appears in Maine and New Hampshire in 1686. Inasmuch as the name Munsey is an uncommon one, it is also likely that the same William was a relative of Francis Munsey of Ipswich, Mass. (1659 to 1664), then of Brookhaven, Long Island; but exactly what the relationship was, we cannot prove.

WILLIAM[1] MUNSEY first appears upon authoritative records in the year 1686, when he signs his name four times as witness to a deed of land in Oyster River (now Durham), N. H., and to addenda thereto. It is interesting to note that of the seven signers, only three could write their names; one of those three was William[1] Munsey, who at that time lived in Kittery, Maine. Not long after, he removed to Dover, N. H., where he followed the cooper's trade. In 1698 he was accidentally drowned in the Piscataqua River. The justice who presided at the inquest was Colonel William[1] Pepperrell, father of the captor of Louisburg. Colonel Pepperrell was a direct ancestor of Andrew Munsey of the fifth generation, and therefore of all of Andrew's descendants. (See Pepperrell family.)

There are numerous indications that William[1] Munsey was a member of the Society of Friends.

His wife's name was Margaret, also a Friend. The possibility that her maiden name was Margaret Clement may be briefly stated thus:

Mr. C. W. Tibbetts, editor of the *New Hampshire Genealogical Register*, has for over fifty years made a study of the families of Dover and vicinity. We enlisted his aid in our research, and after a careful examination of all data he writes:

"I have come to the conclusion that Margaret Munsey was born at Dover in the year 1655; that she was a daughter of Job Clement and his wife Margaret Dummer; that she was granddaughter, on her father's side, of Robert Clement of Haverhill, Mass., and probably was great granddaughter of John Clement—who in 1620 was one of the thirteen Maisters, or Aldermen (as we should call them), of the city of Plymouth, England; that she was granddaughter on her mother's side of Mr. Thomas Dummer of Salisbury, who returned to England and died at Chicknell, North Stoneham, Southampton Co., England, where he probably came from."

Mr. Tibbetts then enters into a rather extended statement of the reasons which lead to his conclusions. His theory is ingenious, but contains at least one false deduction: the father of Robert Clement was *not* John, but Richard (Robert, Robert); and as the maiden name of William[1] Munsey's wife rests on speculative evidence only, we have not included it in the chart. See page 11.

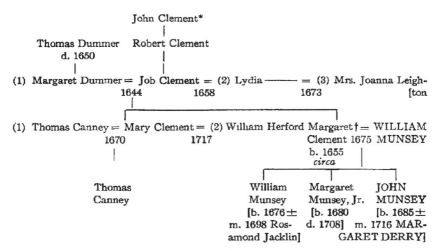

```
                        John Clement*
                             |
      Thomas Dummer    Robert Clement
         d. 1650            |
           |               |
(1) Margaret Dummer = Job Clement = (2) Lydia ——— = (3) Mrs. Joanna Leigh-
           1644         1658            1673                    [ton
                         |
              ┌──────────┴──────────────────────────────┐
(1) Thomas Canney = Mary Clement = (2) William Herford Margaret† = WILLIAM
         1670          1717                        Clement 1675 MUNSEY
           |                                         b. 1655      |
                                                     circa
                                      ┌────────────────┴──────────┐
      Thomas                        William      Margaret      JOHN
      Canney                        Munsey      Munsey, Jr.   MUNSEY
                                  [b. 1676±     [b. 1680      [b. 1685±
                                  m. 1698 Ros-  d. 1708]   m. 1716 MAR-
                                  amond Jacklin]          GARET DERRY]
```

THE TIBBETTS THEORY REGARDING WILLIAM MUNSEY'S WIFE

---

*Later researches (*Essex Inst Hist. Coll.* 53·250) prove that the father of Robert Clement was Richard.
†The will of Job Clement is, however, silent concerning any Margaret (*New Hampshire State Papers*, 31·259).

Apparently WILLIAM[1] and MARGARET MUN-SEY had three children:

1. William[2] Munsey, born 1676±; married, January tenth, 1698/9, Rosamond Jacklin.
2. Margaret[2] Munsey, born 1680; died January twenty-ninth, 1708/9.
3. JOHN[2] MUNSEY, born 1685±; married 1716± MARGARET DERRY; died 1765+.

JOHN[2] MUNSEY and William[2] were certainly brothers, according to the records of their time; that they were the sons of William[1] of Kittery there is no doubt, although no records have been found as direct proof of the fact. John[2]'s name first appears on July third, 1710, when he is enumerated among a band of soldiers in the Indian war, under the command of Col. Hilton. Between 1715 and 1720 he married MARGARET,[2] daughter of JAMES[1] DERRY, and made his home at Oyster River. This was a part of Dover at the first, but became a separate parish in 1716; in 1732 it was incorporated as the township of Durham. The stream upon the boundary between Lee and Durham is spanned by a structure which is still called "Munsey's Bridge."

John[2] Munsey seems to have been a thrifty farmer; he owned land in Durham and Rochester, N. H., and in Kittery, Maine. From 1743-6 he began to part with his possessions by selling his land in Durham to his sons Jonathan[3] and David[3]. In 1761, by a deed in which he styles himself "Brother and only Heir of William Munsey," he conveys a "Twenty Acre Grant of Land granted to my said Brother by the Town of Kittery" in 1694. In 1763 he appears for the last time in the record, when he sells his land in Rochester. In these various transactions he netted about seven hundred pounds.

The few details of John[2] Munsey's life which we possess show him to have been a soldier upon occasion, but a farmer by preference; a family man, a hardy pioneer, and a good neighbor. So far as we know, he had only three children:

1. Jonathan[3] Munsey, born about 1718; migrated to Wiscasset, Me.

2. DAVID[3] MUNSEY, born about 1720; married ABIGAIL[4] PITMAN; died 1801+.

3. Rachel Munsey, born about 1722.

The three children were all baptized by the Rev. Hugh Adams, of Oyster River parish, on January 7, 1727/8.

DAVID[3] MUNSEY was the second son of JOHN[2] MUNSEY (WILLIAM[1]) and M A R G A R E T[2] DERRY (JAMES[1]). David[3]'s name is first recorded in the account of the baptism just mentioned, January 7, 1727/8. He was then probably about seven years of age. On attaining his majority, he bought land near his father; in 1746 he also purchased a part of the homestead "in the Place Commonly Called Newton plains, by Newton road that leads to Barrington." He married ABIGAIL[4] PITMAN (ZACHARIAH[3], JOSEPH[2], WILLIAM[1]), who lived in that part of Dover now called Madbury.

The records show that David[3] Munsey added to his holdings from time to time, both in Durham, Barrington, and Madbury. In 1765/6 the residents of Durham living in the western part of the town petitioned the legislature to set them off as a separate township; among the petitioners occurs the name of David Munsey. This petition was granted, and the township of Lee was formed.

For about ten years history is silent concerning David.[3] Those were stirring time in the New England colonies. In 1776 we find the Association Test spoken of in New Hampshire. This seems to have been designed to show how many were in favor of setting up a temporary government independent of the mother country. In January, New Hampshire actually did declare its independence, six months before the famous Declaration in Independence Hall, Philadelphia. Many of the inhabitants of Lee signed the Association Test, among them David[3]'s son Timothy[4], who later enlisted in the army. But David[3] held aloof. It does not, however, follow that David[3] was opposed to the idea of independence. He may, inheriting a horror of war from his presumed Quaker grandfather, have declined on purely conscientious grounds.

In 1783 Zachariah[3] Pitman, of Madbury, the father of David[3]'s wife, died. In his will of June 3, he leaves property to "my daughter Abigail Munsey, wife of David Munsey." The Pitmans mingled their blood in two streams with that of the Munseys; Abigail's grandfather Joseph[2] Pitman had a brother Nathaniel[2], whose granddaughter Mary[4] was the wife of Abigail's son, Timothy[4] Munsey (see chart).

By the close of the century the sands of David[3]'s life were nearly run. In the year 1800, when he was about fourscore, he sold to David[4] Munsey "the whole of my homestead farm in Lee which I now live on." Elsewhere we find that this comprised about seventy acres, and one-eighth of the Newton sawmill. In 1801 we find both David[3] and David[4] engaged in real estate transactions. In 1803 "David, Jr." is mentioned; this implies that his father is still living.

We find no record of the death of David[3], but in 1807 one David Munsey, of Lee, is appointed administrator of an estate. It is not likely that a man nearly ninety years old would be appointed to that office; and since David[4] is no longer called "Junior," we infer that the elder David[3] was then dead.

The children of David[3] Munsey were:

1. David[4] Munsey, died in Madbury, 1830.±
2. Solomon[4] Munsey, born 1745; had 13 children; died 1827, at Barnstead, New Hampshire.
3. TIMOTHY[4] MUNSEY, born 1749; married 1772, MARY[4] PITMAN; died 1832 in Barnstead, New Hampshire.
4. Henry[4] Munsey, born 1736; died after 1825, at Barnstead, New Hampshire; married Molly Simpson, sister or aunt of General U. S. Grant's grandfather.
5. Abigail[4] Munsey, died in Madbury after 1834.

TIMOTHY[4] MUNSEY (DAVID[3], JOHN[2], WILLIAM[1]) was born in the year 1749. His mother's name, as we have already seen, was ABIGAIL[4] PITMAN (ZACHARIAH[3], JOSEPH[2], WILLIAM[1]). It is quite likely that she named her boy for friendship's sake. A family of Perkinses, in Barrington, just across the Lee line, were neighbors to the Munseys. In that family the name Timothy occurred in two, and perhaps three, generations, and in both families the name Jonathan is found.

In 1772, TIMOTHY[4] MUNSEY married MARY[4] PITMAN (DERRY[3], NATHANIEL[2], WILLIAM[1]) and settled in Lee. His wife had a twin brother, Andrew Pepperrell Pitman. The great-uncle of the twins was the famous Sir William[2] Pepperrell (or Pepperell), hero of Louisburg, Lieutenant-General in the British army, Commissioner to the Indians of New England, President of the Massachusetts Council, and Governor of the Province. His sister JOANNA[2] married DR. GEORGE[2] JACKSON, and their daughter DOROTHY[3] was MARY[4] PITMAN'S mother (see chart). In his last will and testament, Sir William[2] left a small legacy to his niece, DOROTHY[3] PITMAN.

In 1776, as we have already seen, with several others of the inhabitants of Lee, Timothy[4] Munsey signed the Association Test, thus showing his sympathy with the American cause. Later we find, in the Revolutionary Rolls of the State, that in September and October of 1777 he was a soldier in Captain George Tuttle's company, in Colonel Stephen Evans's regiment of New Hampshire militia. This regiment later joined the Continental Army under General Gates at Saratoga; but before this, there was some trouble between the privates and their superior officers, and all of Timothy[4]'s company seem to have gone on a strike, returning to their homes *en masse*.

Three years later, we find Timothy[4] living in Durham and buying "one-third of 200 Acres" for twenty pounds. In 1786 he still resides in Durham as a "husbandman," but sells "one-third of 100 Ac.

of land in Northfield," thirty-five to forty miles distant, to one Jos. Leavitt, Jr., for twelve pounds. How he became possessed of that distant lot, we cannot tell; we do know, however, that at the same time he was an important taxpayer in Durham. But after the year 1786 the name of Munsey disappears from the Durham tax-list, for Timothy[4] and his family removed to Barnstead.

The old Munsey farm in Barnstead was at a place where two roads cross, hence termed Munsey's Corner. Later, diagonally opposite the farm buildings, a large schoolhouse was erected, always known as the Munsey schoolhouse. It was used as a place of worship, also, for many years; "good old Parson George" was accustomed to preach there both forenoon, afternoon, and at early candle-lighting every third Sabbath.

In the year 1904 Mr. Horace N. Colbath, a prominent resident of Barnstead, wrote as follows in reply to our inquiries:

Timothy[4] Munsey settled in Barnstead, New Hampshire, immediately after the close of the Revolutionary War, near the Munsey Corner, which name it now retains, although there has been no family of the name living near there for over forty years; there were no roads in that part of the town when he built his log house and moved his family there.

My grandfather, John Colbath, owned the lot west of the Munsey lot, and made a clearing adjoining. When the road was built. it was found that a part of Munsey's clearing was on my grandfather's lot, and my grandfather cleared a like area for Munsey.

I have known the Munsey family sixty-five years, was guardian for one in his old age, and was executor or administrator of the estates of three other members of the family. They were strong in their likes and dislikes; were witty and generous; and always had the courage of their convictions, and an abiding faith in their opnions, no matter what the world might say.

On January 9, 1832, Timothy[4] Munsey died intestate. His son Ebenezer was appointed administrator, under bonds of four thousand dollars. From the Strafford County records we find the following appraisal of his estate:

Farm of 60 acres	$1,300.00
Wood lot of 20 acres	200.00
Plains land—5 acres	330.00
Personal estate	335.01
	$2,165.01

It is interesting to note that a horse was appraised at $50.00, a yoke of oxen at $58.00, a cow at $12.00 and a sheep at $1.88. By comparing these prices with the values of such animals to-day, we discover that the estate, both real and personal, was much more valuable than the figures would indicate.

It is evident that the Barnstead heirs of Timothy[4] Munsey empowered the administrator to buy out the claims of others. A quitclaim deed is on record in Strafford County signed by Andrew Munsey, Jedediah and Polly Hall, and John and Catherine Beck, all of Sandwich, N. H., relinquishing to Ebenezer Munsey of Barnstead, for the sum of five hundred dollars cash, "the homestead farm of Timothy Munsey, of said Barnstead, deceased." Then follows the full description of the estate. It seems likely, from the foregoing, that Polly Hall and Catherine Beck were sisters of Ebenezer[5], Sarah[5], Jane[5], and Andrew[5] Munsey.

Mr. Woodbury Munsey, of Barnstead, N. H., told the writer in 1904 that Timothy[4] Munsey was the earliest settler in the town; that he came from Durham; and that later two brothers, Solomon[4] and Henry[4], and a sister, Abigail[4], followed him.

TIMOTHY[4] and MARY[4] (PITMAN) MUNSEY had the following children:

1. Ebenezer[5] Munsey, born 1773; married Mary Vinal of Maine; died 1853.
2. Sarah[5] Munsey, born 1780; married Henry Nutter of Barnstead; died —— ——.
3. Jane[5] Munsey, born —— ——; died unmarried.
4. ANDREW[5] MUNSEY (named evidently from his mother's twin brother, Andrew Pepperrell Pitman), born 1785; married (1) Mary Bartlett; (2) BETSEY[6] SAWYER, 1812; died 1853.

probably also

5. Polly[5] Munsey, born —— —— ——; married Jedidiah Hall of Sandwich.
6. Catherine[5] Munsey, born —— —— ——; married John Beck of Sandwich.

In the old Munsey burying-ground, a little way from Munsey Corner, stands the gravestone of Timothy[4] Munsey and his wife. The former died in 1832, at the age of 83; the latter in 1830, aged 80.

ANDREW[5] MUNSEY (TIMOTHY[4], DAVID[3], JOHN[2], WILLIAM[1]) was born, according to the affidavit of his son, in the state of New Hampshire, in the year 1785. While he was still a young man, he went to the vicinity of Wiscasset, Maine, whither his great uncle Jonathan[3] had preceded him many years before. He married (1) Mary Bartlett, of Montville; their only child, Mary Bartlett[6] Munsey became the wife of Orchard Rowell, and lived at or near Rockland, Maine. Mrs. Munsey soon died, and not long after this her husband enlisted in the war of 1812.

We next find ANDREW[5] MUNSEY in the little town of Stark, Somerset County, Maine. There he marries (2) BETSEY[6], the daughter of GEORGE[5], SAWYER (AHOLIAB[4], WILLIAM[3], THOMAS[2], THOMAS[1]). Since Sawyer himself was a soldier of 1812, it may be that the two men became acquainted in the army.

The children of Andrew[5] Munsey's second marriage were as follows:

1. Rhoda[6] Munsey, born about 1813, in Stark; died young.
2. Timothy[6] Munsey, born 1814, in Stark; died in Lowell, Mass., 1868 (or 1873).
3. Lucy Merritt[6] Munsey, born 1816, in Barnstead, N. H.; married Abel Young; died in 1903.
4. George Washington[6] Munsey, born 1819, in Barnston, Quebec; died in 1900.
5. ANDREW CHAUNCEY[6] MUNSEY, born 1821, in Barnston, Quebec; married (1), in 1847, **MARY JANE MERRITT[6] HOPKINS**; (2) in 1883, Mrs. Mary Morse (Atwood) Cutting; died in 1907.
6. Betsey (Lizzie) Amanda Jane[6] Munsey, born 1828, in Barnston, Quebec; married Jonathan Young; died in 1863.

From the fact that Lucy M. Munsey was born in Barnstead, we see that Andrew[5] Munsey had left Stark and was back in Barnstead; either resident there, or possibly visiting his father and mother. We next find him in Barnston, Quebec, where three children were born; but other records locate him in Sandwich, N. H., in 1833.

In 1848 Betsey[6] (Sawyer) Munsey died, and was buried in Smithfield, Maine. Andrew[5] Munsey continued to reside in Canada, where he died April 30,

1853, and was buried in Barnston; later his remains were removed to Smithfield and buried beside those of his wife Betsey.

ANDREW CHAUNCEY[6] MUNSEY (ANDREW[5], TIMOTHY[4], DAVID[3], JOHN[2], WILLIAM[1]) was the fifth child and third son of Andrew[5] Munsey by his second wife, Betsey[6] Sawyer. In our search we find that there was a Charles Chauncey, of Kittery, living with the Pepperrell family and related to them, who had a son Andrew Chauncey. Now as we recall that Andrew Munsey was doubtless named for his uncle, Andrew Pepperrell Pitman, he seems, in calling his son Andrew Chauncey Munsey, to have made a deliberate attempt to connect the Pepperrell-Chauncey and the Pitman-Munsey families by means of the common link, Andrew. (See chart.)

Andrew Chauncey[6] Munsey was born June 13, 1821. When he was twelve years of age, he went to New Hampshire, where he spent his boyhood. On attaining his majority he went to Maine: first to Smithfield, to visit his mother's people; then to Lincoln, a town about fifty miles north of Bangor. Five years later he married his first wife, MARY JANE MERRITT[8] HOPKINS (ELISHA[7], ELISHA[6], SIMEON[5], CALEB[4], CALEB[3], GILES[2], STEPHEN[1],—the last two *Mayflower passengers*),—of Litchfield, Me. (See Hopkins Line.)

To them were born three daughters, Ella Augusta[7], Emma Jane[7], and Mary[7]. Then in 1853 the Munseys bought a farm in Mercer, Maine, a town adjoining Smithfield, the home of the Sawyers, Mr. Munsey's maternal ancestors. Here in 1854, on August 21, **FRANK ANDREW**[7] **MUNSEY** was born. Six months later his father moved to Gardiner, Maine; three years after this he bought a farm in the town of Bowdoin, and removed thither. Here **FRANK ANDREW**[7] lived until he was fourteen years of age, doing real work on the farm, laying the foundation for the future, and forming the habits which have characterized his life.

In 1868 ANDREW C.[6] MUNSEY moved to Lisbon Falls, Maine; about ten years later he went to Livermore Falls, Maine, where he resided the remainder of his life, dying in 1907, on July 1.

In 1858, when ANDREW C.[6] was residing in Bowdoin, another daughter was born, Delia Mary[7]; and in 1861, also in Bowdoin, another son, William Cushing.[7] In 1882, on August 23, MR. MUNSEY'S **WIFE** died; she was buried at Lisbon Falls in the family burying-ground. In November, 1883, MR. MUNSEY again married, this time Mrs. Mary Morse (Atwood) Cutting.

ANDREW C[6]. MUNSEY'S life was spent as a farmer and a builder, except for three years, which he gave up to the Civil War, being a member of the Twentieth Maine Regiment. The writer knew MR. ANDREW C.[6] MUNSEY well. He was a man of strong qualities and rugged honesty. He was rigid in his opinions. His was an intense nature, and he was a very hard worker. Idleness to him was intolerable. In a word, ANDREW CHAUNCEY[6] MUNSEY had the grit, the confidence, and the courage to have done important things if he had had the opportunity in early life, before he took upon himself the responsibilities of caring for a large family.

AUTHORITIES

As stated in the Preface, most of the authorities by which the Munsey Line is proved are in manuscript deeds, wills, records, and affidavits, of which the originals or certified copies have been secured by patient research. One printed authority, however, to which we would refer the reader, is the "History of Durham, New Hampshire" (Stackpole and Meserve, 1914, Vol. 2, pp. 294-296).

PART II
THE HOPKINS LINE

In PART II all Hopkins names printed in red are those
of direct ancestors of Frank A. Munsey on his
mother's side; direct maternal ancestors
outside the Hopkins Line are printed
in large black CAPITALS.

PART II
THE HOPKINS LINE

The history of the Hopkins L i n e f r o m STEPHEN[1], to MARY JANE MERRITT[8], eight generations, we will now briefly unroll.

In Pilgrim Hall, Plymouth, Mass., there is a painting by Henry Sargent, a Boston artist, a member of the family to which the celebrated John Singer Sargent belongs. Among the figures there appearing on the canvas is a group representing STEPHEN HOPKINS, his wife, and four children.

1. STEPHEN[1] HOPKINS is said by some to have been a London merchant. He was one of the twelve *Mayflower* passengers who had a title (Mr.)* prefixed to his name. His party consisted of a second wife, Elizabeth; two children by a FORMER WIFE Constance[2] and GILES[2]—the latter a boy of thirteen; a daughter Damaris[2], about two years of age; and a babe Oceanus[2], so named because he was born upon the ocean, in the *Mayflower*. Besides his family, two servants, Edward Leister and Edward Doty, completed his party. What is believed to be the English record of Stephen's second marriage is in St. Mary's, Whitechapel, London. It reads as follows:

Stephen Hopkins et Eliza: ffisher, March, 1617.

---

*Originally an abbreviation of "Master," and "used only of persons of high social rank or learning." The pronunciation of *Mr.* finally changed to "Mister," and the title gradually lost its significance.

27

That Stephen[1] Hopkins was a man of more than ordinary force of character and influence is shown by
the part he played in the early history of the colony.
In Howard and Crocker's "Popular History of New
England" we read: "No one can ponder the annals
of the early settlement of New England without
being profoundly impressed with the rare excellency
of the material that went into its foundation. Consider the names of such primitive Pilgrims as Carver,
Bradford, BREWSTER, Standish, Winslow, AL-
DEN, WARREN, HOPKINS, and others"; and
Moore, in his "Lives of the Colonial Governors,"
says: "Of the Pilgrims who remained in 1634,
STEPHEN HOPKINS, Miles Standish, and JOHN
ALDEN were the most prominent individuals.
Hopkins was then one of the principal magis-
trates."

STEPHEN[1] HOPKINS was not only one of the
first men among the Pilgrims, but he had extraor-
dinary fortune in being concerned with many of the
first things that happened to the colonists, whether
for good or for evil. Thus, he was one of the signers
of the first Declaration of Independence in the New
World—the famous Compact, drawn up and signed
in the cabin of the *Mayflower*, November twenty-
first, 1620; it has been called "the nucleus around
which everything else clustered—unquestionably the
foundation of all the superstructures of government
which have since been reared in these United States."
He was a member of the first expedition that left the
ship to find a place for landing ("ten of our men were
appointed who were of themselves willing to under-

take it"); he was in the first party that went ashore at Plymouth Rock; he was the first white man of the colony to entertain an Indian at his house over night; he went (with Gov. Winslow and Squantum) on the first embassy sent to Massasoit to conclude a treaty; he was a member of the first Council of Governor's Assistants after the incorporation of Plymouth— a position to which he was chosen for three years in succession (1632-1635); and to this we may add that his two servants, Edward Leister and Edward Doty, fought the first duel on record in New England.

There is much additional evidence to show that STEPHEN[1] HOPKINS bulked large in the early life of the Plymouth Colony. He heads a list of persons chosen to arrange for trade with outsiders— a sort of incipient chamber of commerce; he is added to the Governor and Assistants in 1637 as an Assessor to raise a fund for sending aid to the Massachusetts Bay and Connecticut colonies in the impending Indian war; and in the same year he and his two sons, GILES[2] and Caleb[2] (three Hopkinses; more than of any other name), are among the forty-two who volunteered their services as soldiers to aid these same colonies—a fact in noteworthy contrast with the statement of three carpet knights: that they will "goe if they be prest." We find him repeatedly mentioned as an appraiser of estates, administrator, guardian, juryman (foreman, apparently), etc. In 1638 "liberty was granted" him "to erect a house at Mattacheese (or Mattakeese, i. e., Yarmouth) and cutt hay there this yeare to winter his cattle— provided, that it be not to withdraw him from the town of Plymouth." He was too valuable a citizen to lose.

He seems to have been fairly prosperous, withal; for toward the close of his life we find him purchasing a share in a vessel of 40 to 50 tons, valued at two hundred pounds sterling.

On June 6, 1644, he made his will. The exact date of his death is unknown; but it must have been before July 17, for then his inventory was taken. The will was witnessed by ("exhibited upon the Oathes of") Gov. Bradford and Capt. Standish. In this he passes by his oldest son, GILES², and makes Caleb², the only son of his second wife, his heir and executor.

The children of STEPHEN¹ HOPKINS were as follows:—

By his FIRST WIFE,——————————

1. Constance² Hopkins, born in England about 1605; married 1623/4 Nicholas Snow.
2. GILES² HOPKINS, born in England about 1607; married 1639; died 1690.

By his second wife (Elizabeth Fisher?)

1. Damaris² Hopkins, born in England before 1619. (She probably died young; see below).
2. Oceanus² Hopkins, born 1620 on the *Mayflower*, died before June first, 1627.
3. Caleb² Hopkins, born in Plymouth before 1623; died unmarried in Barbadoes, before 1651.
4. Deborah² Hopkins, born perhaps 1625; married Andrew Ring.
5. Damaris² Hopkins 2d, born perhaps 1627; married, after 1646, Jacob Cooke (if the first Damaris died).
6. Ruth² Hopkins, evidently died unmarried.
7. Elizabeth² Hopkins, probably died unmarried.

2. GILES[2] HOPKINS (STEPHEN[1]) of Plymouth, Yarmouth, and Eastham, was the son of Stephen's FIRST WIFE, whose name is unknown. He
was born in England about 1607, and came over with
his father in the *Mayflower*. His own sister, Constance[2], seems to have been his senior; she married
Nicholas Snow at some time between 1623 and 1627.
GILES[2] remained unmarried until October 9, 1639,
when he took to wife CATHERINE (or Catorne, as
he calls her in his will), daughter of GABRIEL
WHELDEN (or WHELDON), of Yarmouth, who
bore him ten children. Shortly before his marriage
he removed from Plymouth to Yarmouth (Mattakeese), where we find him highway surveyor in
1642-1643, and where he was living at the time of his
father's death in 1644. A few years later he went
to Eastham (Nauset), and in 1655 he was one of
the 29 legal voters* there. He died there an octo-
genarian.

In 1682 GILES[2] evidently believed himself near his
end; for on the 19th of January he made his will,
styling himself "sick and weak of Body and yet of
perfit memory." In this will he bequeaths property
to his wife and his four living sons (Stephen[3], CALEB[3],
Joshua[3], and William[3]), but makes no mention of his
daughters (Mary[3], Abigail[3], Deborah[3], and Ruth[3]).
It would seem that William was an invalid, for
GILES[2] wills that "my son Stephen Hopkins shall
take ye care and oversight and maintain my son
William Hopkins during his natural Life in a com-

---

*A legal voter was a male citizen who had attained his
majority (21 years) and, in the early Colonial days, had been
made a freeman. See footnote under Aborn, page 50.

fortable and decent manner." With great sim-
plicity GILES² then decides that Joshua³ shall outlive
not only his mother but also his brother William³;
for, after willing "too acres of meadow" to "Catorne
and william" during their lives, he adds:—

"And after ye decease of my wife and son william
I do give this above sd too acres of meadow to my
son Joshua Hopkins and his heirs forever."

GILES² HOPKINS lived about eight years after
the making of the will, and finally became so feeble
that he added a codicil giving "all my stock and
moveable estate" to Stephen³ in return for mine and
my wife's Comfortable Support." He apparently
passed away in the early part of 1690. His children
by CATHERINE WHELDEN, who probably survived him, were as follows:

1. Mary³ Hopkins, born November, 1640; married January third, 1665, Samuel Smith.
2. Stephen³ Hopkins, born September, 1642; married May
twenty-third, 1667, Mary Merrick.
3. John³ Hopkins, born 1643; died at age of three months.
4. Abigail³ Hopkins, born October, 1644; married May
twenty-third, 1667, William Merrick.
5. Deborah³ Hopkins, born June, 1648; married July
second, 1668, Josiah Cooke.
6. CALEB³ HOPKINS, born January, 1650/1; married
MARY WILLIAMS; died 1728.
7. Ruth³ Hopkins, born June, 1653.
8. Joshua³ Hopkins, born June, 1657; married May twenty-
sixth, 1681, Mary Cole.
9. William³ Hopkins, born January ninth, 1660.
10. Elizabeth Hopkins, born November, 1664; died at age
of one month.

3. CALEB³ HOPKINS (GILES², STEPHEN¹), of
Eastham and Truro, was the sixth child and third

son of GILES[2] and CATHERINE[2] (WHELDEN) HOPKINS. He was born at Eastham in January, 1650/1, and died intestate, probably not long before May twenty-second, 1728, when his son, CALEB[4], was appointed administrator. The wife of CALEB[3] was MARY[2] WILLIAMS, daughter of THOMAS[1] WILLIAMS, of Eastham, who in his will of May tenth, 1692, mentions a daughter, MARY HOPKINS. She must have died before her husband, as there is no mention of a widow in the settlement of the estate of CALEB[3]. No record has been found of the marriage of CALEB[3] HOPKINS and MARY[2] WILLIAMS, or of the birth of CALEB[4]; yet ample evidence exists that MARY was the wife of CALEB[3], and that CALEB[4] was their "eldest son." Since Nathaniel, their "second son," was probably at least 21 years old at the time of his marriage to Mercy Mayo, in 1707, he must have been born as early as 1686; then CALEB[4] was probably born as early as 1684. That would make him 57 at the time of his death in 1741. He was not born previous to January nineteenth, 1682, for his grandfather, GILES[2], in his will drawn on that date says, "if either of my sons, Joshua or CALEB [the father of CALEB[4]] dye having no Issew, etc." Joshua[3] was at that time married to Mary Cole, and probably also CALEB[3] to MARY WILLIAMS; but from the foregoing passage we see that neither of them then had children.

The name of CALEB[3] HOPKINS appears in the first entry in the first book of records in the possession of the town of Truro. It bears date June 17,

1690, and shows that CALEB HOPKINS and six others were then proprietors of Pamet (Truro).

In the Agreement of the Heirs of CALEB³ HOPKINS, made on June fifth, 1728, we find the following children named:—

1. CALEB⁴ HOPKINS, "eldest son," born about 1684, who married MERCY FREEMAN in 1719.

2. Nathaniel⁴ Hopkins, "second son," who married Mercy Mayo in 1707.

3. Thomas⁴ Hopkins, "third son," who married Deborah

4. Thankful⁴ Hopkins, "only daughter," born Truro, May twenty-seventh, 1709; married Ambrose Dyer in 1729.

The first article of the agreement reads as follows:

1. In the first place tis Mutually Agreed that CALEB HOPKINS Eldest son of said CALEB HOPKINS Deceased his heirs and Assigns forever shall have hold And possess over and Above what his Late father Conveyed to him by deed of gift in his Life time, One Lot of Land that Lyeth on the south westerly side of the high way that goeth up from the pond to the Meeting house in said Town and Joyns to the Land of Mʳ· Moses Paine, and one third part of all the Marsh which his said Father did Not Legally Dispose of in his Life time—

The second article agrees that certain lands shall fall to Nathaniel⁴ Hopkins ("being the second son of the said Deceased"); the third article states that certain lands and one half the personal estate, "except the Debts Due his said Late father," shall fall to Thomas⁴ Hopkins, the third son; and the fourth article, that other lands and the other half of the personal estate, except debts as aforesaid, shall fall to Thankful⁴ Hopkins ("being the only Daughter of the said Deceased").

Finally it was "Mutually Agreed that all the debts Due from our said Late father as well Charges as

alsoe by his sickness and funerall and for the Settlement of this said Estate be paid Equally Divided
amongst us all (That is to Say) Each One shall have
a quarter part thereof."

4. CALEB[4] HOPKINS (CALEB[3], GILES[2],
STEPHEN[1]) was probably born, as we have seen,
about 1684, in Truro. He married in Truro, October eighth, 1719, MERCY[4] FREEMAN (CON-
STANT[3], SAMUEL[2], SAMUEL[1]), who was born
in Eastham (Nauset), August thirty-first, 1702, and
died in December, 1786.

Very little is known of CALEB[4]'S life, except that
he seems to have been a prosperous farmer. The
Truro records show that on February 16, 1730, he
was chosen on a committee of thirty-six proprietors
to look to the preservation of the meadows of the
township. He died intestate in 1741. On October
21 his oldest son Constant[5] of Truro, yeoman, ap-
plied to be appointed administrator. The inventory
of his estate, taken November twenty-fourth, 1741,
showed property amounting to six hundred seventy-
one pounds, twelve shillings sterling (about $3,358).
On the tenth of March following (1741/2) an allow-
ance was made to his widow MERCY and "severall
small children" (six were then under fourteen years
of age), and the full account was rendered by the
Administrator, Constant[5].

The children of CALEB[4] and MERCY[4] (FREE-
MAN) HOPKINS were:

   1. Constant[5] Hopkins, born Truro, July twenty-eighth,

baptized August twenty-first, 1720; married December first, 1743, Phoebe, daughter of Jonathan Paine.

2. Mary[6] Hopkins, born Truro July eighteenth, baptized July twenty-second, 1722; married October twenty-first, 1747, John Cross, of Boston.

3. Thankful[6] Hopkins, born Truro May thirtieth, baptized June twenty-eighth, 1724; married (1) June twelfth, 1746, Elisha Paine, born 1721; (2) 1757, Freeman Higgins.

4. Caleb[6] Hopkins, born Truro July twenty-eighth, baptized July thirty-first, 1726; married (1) January fourth, 1747, Mary Paine; (2) June fifteenth, 1777, Jane Vernon; (3) March twenty-second, 1781, Mary Williams. He was a banker in Boston.

5. Jonathan[6] Hopkins, born Truro, July twenty-seventh, baptized August twenty-fifth, 1728; died at sea.

6. SIMEON[5] HOPKINS, born Truro, February seventh, baptized March twelfth, 1731/2; married August twenty-eighth, 1755, BETTY COBB, of Truro. Moved to Maine after 1760.

7. Mercy[6] Hopkins, born Truro April twenty-sixth, baptized May twenty-sixth, 1734; married, about 1758, John Grozier. Lived in Truro.

8. James[6] Hopkins, born Truro August sixteenth, baptized September nineteenth, 1736; married Mehitable Freeman; settled in Middletown, Conn.

9. John[6] Hopkins, born Truro January tenth, baptized February fourth, 1738/9; died at sea.

10. Abiel[6] Hopkins, born Truro August twenty-first, baptized September twenty-seventh, 1741; is recorded as a child of MERCY HOPKINS. This would imply that the father CALEB[4] died before August twenty-first. We have already seen that he died in 1741. Nothing more is known of Abiel.

5. SIMEON[5] HOPKINS, of Truro, Massachusetts, and Brunswick and Harpswell, Maine (CALEB[4-3], GILES[2], STEPHEN[1]), was born February seventh and baptized March twelfth, 1731/2, in Truro, Massachusetts. He married, August twenty-eighth, 1755, BETTY[4] COBB (THOMAS[3], RICHARD[2], THOMAS[1]), who was born December twenty-second, 1732, and was living March fifth,

1812. They both owned the covenant October seventeenth, 1756. The date of SIMEON[5]'S death is unknown; he was living as late as September first, 1821.

SIMEON[5] and BETTY[4] (COBB) HOPKINS had five children, three of whom were born in Truro; they were:

1. Mercy[6] Hopkins, born August sixth, baptized October seventeenth, 1756; married May sixteenth, 1776, Reuben Higgins.

2. Simeon[6] Hopkins, born March eleventh, baptized May seventh, 1758.

3. James[6] Hopkins, born August thirty-first, baptized November sixteenth, 1760. A James Hopkins was lost at sea near the Grand Banks in 1818; possibly it was this James.

About the year 1760, SIMEON[5] and his WIFE moved to the State (then the province) of Maine. Their two youngest children were:

4. ELISHA[6] HOPKINS, born, perhaps, 1762; married, May sixteenth, 1784, REBECCA[2] MEREEN; lived in Harpswell.

5. Betsey[6] Hopkins, born, perhaps, 1764; married April tenth, 1783, Henry Totman.

For a long time we were unable to find any trace of SIMEON[5] or his family after the year 1760. All the vital records of Truro and the Cape towns are silent, as if the sea had swallowed him up; and in a sense it doubtless had. A reasonable explanation of his sudden disappearance, and of the fact that we found it so difficult to trace him, is: he was a seafaring man, and doubtless on one of his voyages he took his little family with him down to Maine and found there a place which suited him better than the region of Cape Cod. This theory receives confirmation by the discovery of a record in the Cumberland County

(Maine) Registry of Deeds—now burned—to the effect that SIMEON HOPKINS, mariner, of Brunswick, Maine, on April 14, 1762, for £73 6s. 8d., buys of Samuel Thompson land on Sebascodegan (Great Island), Harpswell, Maine, being Lot No. 22, containing 100 acres more or less. Two more children were born to SIMEON[5] after his removal to Maine, ELISHA[6] and Betsey[6].

During the Revolutionary War, in 1775, we find the name of SIMEON HOPKINS on the important Committee of Inspection and Correspondence for Brunswick and Harpswell; this was undoubtedly SIMEON[5] then about 44 years of age, for Simeon[6], his son, was only 17 at the time. Five years later we again find SIMEON HOPKINS on the Committee of Correspondence. This may have been the younger Simeon[6], as he was then 22; but it is more likely that his father was chosen, because of his previous experience.

When SIMEON[5] and BETTY HOPKINS were about 80 years of age (5 March, 1812), they sold their farm on Sebascodegan, together with their stock and personal estate and another small island near by, for 1500 (dollars). The purchasers were ELISHA[6] HOPKINS and his two sons, ELISHA[7] and Simeon[7]. The last named was then a resident of Lincoln; as he is called Simeon, Jr., it is probable that his uncle Simeon[6] had died—perhaps in the war. Nine years later we have reason to believe that the wife and son (ELISHA[6]) of SIMEON[5] had both died; for ELISHA[7] sells to Simeon[7], his brother, his undivided half of the aforesaid Lot No. 22 on Sebascodegan,

which the boys and their father (ELISHA[6]) had purchased of SIMEON[5], But whereas they paid $1,500,
ELISHA[7] sells his half to Simeon[7] for only $400 on
the following conditions: *"and I, the said Simeon
Hopkins, Junr., do agree to maintain my Grand-
Father SIMEON[5] HOPKINS during his Natrel life
and pay all charges that may occur."*

6. ELISHA[6] HOPKINS, of Harpswell, Maine,
(SIMEON[5], CALEB[4-3], GILES[2], STEPHEN[1]) was
probably born in Harpswell about 1762. He married in that town, May sixteenth, 1784, REBECCA[2],
daughter of LIEUT. JOHN[1] MEREEN; she died
about 1854, at the age of 92. The date of ELISHA[6]'S
death has not been found; but we have already
shown that it probably occurred before 1821, when
he was less than 60 years old.

In Wheeler's "History of Brunswick, Topsham,
and Harpswell," ELISHA[6] HOPKINS is called a
"privateersman." This allusion is probably to a
bold adventure in which young ELISHA[6] was a par-
ticipator during the Revolutionary War, before his
marriage. From the history just referred to we con-
dense and adapt the following account:

In the year 1782, or perhaps a little earlier,
ELISHA[6] HOPKINS and a few other men of Sebascodegan Island, Harpswell, took part in a daring and
successful exploit. For some years, small schooners,
"tenders" to the English men-of-war, had been play-
ing the part of pirates toward the defenseless farmers
and fishermen of Casco Bay. At last the victims
determined upon reprisals. They knew that one of

the crews of these piratical schooners was wont to
land at Condy's Harbor, on Sebascodegan, and they
planned to capture both the vessel and its crew.

Watch was kept, and one day word went forth
that the *Picaroon* had landed at Condy's; accordingly all who were willing to attempt her capture
were summoned to meet at Col. Nathaniel Purinton's that evening, at 10 P. M. Thirty brave fellows
responded, among them young ELISHA HOPKINS,
then only eighteen or twenty years of age. Stealth-
ily they crept toward the vessel; but when they
reached the dock they found she had slipped her
moorings and put out to sea. About twenty resolved
to go in pursuit, with such means as they could
command; so they borrowed of Isaac Snow his
fishing boat, the *Shavingmill*, of only eight tons, and
started forth, rowing and sailing. Snow went with
them as second officer, under Col. Purinton, in
command. At Small Point they found a larger boat,
the *America*, and exchanged; here, like Gideon's
band, they left two or three of their number who
were disposed to show the white feather.

At sunrise of the following morning they sighted
the *Picaroon* off Seguin in the act of capturing a
coaster, to which she transferred her two three-
pounder swivel-guns. With these the English crew
opened fire upon the *America* as she drew near.
But Col. Purinton ordered his men to lie low and say
nothing till they were within pistol shot; then,
at the word, they rose in groups and poured in a
withering fire, meanwhile coming to close quarters
and grappling with the enemy.

Quickly the islanders poured over the coaster's rail. They found one dead man on the deck, one more severely wounded, and five badly scared Britishers hiding in the hold. With the *Picaroon*, the coaster, eight prisoners, two swivel-guns, and some ammunition, Col. Purinton and his "privateersmen" then sailed for Condy's Harbor, where they landed just twenty hours after they had set out. ELISHA[6] HOPKINS'S share of the prize money was at the rate of $1.00 per hour. So far as we know, this was the last of ELISHA'S experience as a soldier or sailor. A few years later we find him a family man, engaged in rearing and training the following children:

1. ELISHA[7] HOPKINS, born March thirtieth, 1788, at Bowdoin or Harpswell, Maine; married August thirteenth, 1812, at Phippsburg, MIRIAM[7], daughter of WILLIAM[6] SPRAGUE; died August eighth, 1870, at Litchfield Plains.

2. Simeon[7] Hopkins, born 1791, married (1) 1819, Margaret Raymond. (2) January fifth, 1821, Mary Raymond.

3. Samuel[7] Hopkins, born 1800; married October twenty-fourth, 1824, Abigail Raymond; died January eighteenth, 1859.

4. Rebecca[7] Hopkins, married, 1825, William Tarr of Bowdoin, Maine.

5. John[7] Hopkins, lost at sea.

6. Polly[7] Hopkins, married Benj. Blanchard.

7. ELISHA[7] HOPKINS of Bowdoin(?), Harpswell, and Litchfield, Maine (ELISHA[6], SIMEON[5], CALEB[4-3], GILES[2], STEPHEN[1]) was born, according to some in Bowdoin, according to others in Harpswell, Maine, March thirtieth, 1788. He married August thirteenth, 1812, MIRIAM[7] SPRAGUE (WILLIAM[6-5], JETHRO[4], WILLIAM[3], JOHN[2], FRANCIS[1]). She was born at Phippsburg, Maine, March sixteenth, 1792, and died at Lisbon Falls,

January twentieth, 1876. ELISHA[7] HOPKINS died at Litchfield, Maine, August eighth, 1870. He (or possibly his father) was a soldier during the War of 1812, enrolled in Captain Snow's regiment, September, 1814. ELISHA[7] was then 26 years old, and his father, ELISHA[6], about 52. It is possible that the "ELISHA HOPKINS" mentioned is the father, and that he died during the war; for as we have seen Simeon[5] apparently outlived ELISHA[6]. For the purchase of land by ELISHA[6], ELISHA[7], and Simeon[7] and the subsequent arrangement between the two brothers to care for their grandfather, see under SIMEON[5]. The children of ELISHA[7] and MIRIAM[7] (SPRAGUE) HOPKINS were as follows:

1. Elizabeth (Betsey)[8] Hopkins, born at Harpswell, March sixth, 1613; married October thirteenth, 1840, Justin W. True; lived in Lincoln.

2. William Sprague[8] Hopkins, born September eighteenth, 1814; drowned June twenty-third, 1823.

3. Simeon[8] Hopkins, born May fifteenth, 1817; married October thirtieth, 1842, Mary Ann Peacock; died March twenty-fifth, 1856.

4. MARY JANE MERRITT[8] HOPKINS, born in Harpswell, March twenty-seventh, 1820; married, November eighth, 1847, ANDREW CHAUNCEY MUNSEY; died August twenty-third, 1882.

5. John[8] Hopkins, born in Litchfield May fourteenth, 1823; died January tenth, 1854.

6. William Loring[8] Hopkins, born February eleventh, 1825; married (1) Amanda M. Clark, (2) Mary A. Wyman, (3) Lizzie R. Myrick. Moved to Detroit, Maine.

7. James Rogers[8] Hopkins, born in Litchfield, November fifteenth, 1828; married May eighth, 1864, Elmira F. Stall of Bowdoinham; died August eleventh, 1898, at Westbrook, Maine.

8. Samuel Rogers[8] Hopkins, born July twenty-ninth, 1830; married, 1869, Elizabeth Abigail Roberts of Portland; died June twenty-ninth, 1902.

8. MARY JANE MERRITT[8] HOPKINS (ELISHA[7-6], SIMEON[5], CALEB[4-3], GILES[2], STEPHEN[1]) was born on Great Island (Sebascodegan), Harpswell, Maine, March twenty-seventh, 1820; she was married at Litchfield, Maine, November eighth, 1847, to **ANDREW CHAUNCEY**[6] **MUNSEY** (ANDREW[5], TIMOTHY[4], DAVID[3], JOHN[2], WILLIAM[1]); she died at Livermore Falls, August twenty-third, 1882, and was buried at Lisbon Falls, Maine.

MRS. MUNSEY was a woman of sterling worth, highly esteemed by all who knew her. She was of illustrious ancestry on both her paternal and her maternal lines. Her father was a lineal descendant of four *Mayflower* passengers—STEPHEN[1] and GILES[2] HOPKINS, and WILLIAM[1] and MARY BREWSTER; also of *Constant*[1] *Southworth*, *Edmund*[1] and *Maj. John*[2] *Freeman*, and *Lieut. John*[1] *Mereen* of the Revolutionary War; of the *Revs. John*[1] *Mayo* and *Samuel*[2] *Treat*; and of *Govs. Robert*[2] *Treat* and *Thomas*[1] *Prince*. Her mother reckoned among her ancestors no less than eight *Mayflower* passengers—WILLIAM[1], MARY, and LOVE[2] BREWSTER, WILLIAM[1], ALICE, AND PRISCILLA[2] MULLINS, JOHN[1] ALDEN, and RICHARD[1] WARREN. We also find among her forbears the well known names of *Christopher*[1] *Wadsworth*, *Robert*[1] *Bartlett*, *William*[1] *Paybody* (Peabody) and *Lieut. William*[5] *Sprague* of the Revolutionary War. The male descendants of Lieut. Sprague are eligible, under certain regulations, to the Order of the Cincinnati.

MRS. MUNSEY had moved with her father in early childhood (1822 or 1823) from Harpswell to Litchfield. After her marriage she lived in Lincoln, Gardiner, Litchfield, Mercer, Gardiner again, Bowdoin, Lisbon Falls, and Livermore Falls. She was a rare helpmeet to her husband, adapting herself, with rare tact, to his desires and needs. She profoundly impressed her children, training them up in the ways of integrity and righteousness. Her memory was ever revered by both husband and offspring.

ANDREW C.[6] and MARY J. M.[8] (HOPKINS) MUNSEY had the following children:

1. Ella Augusta[7] Munsey, born in Lincoln, September fifth, 1848; died at Lisbon Falls, May twenty-first, 1872.

2. Emma Jane[7] Munsey, born in Gardiner, March seventeenth, 1850; married November twenty-eighth, 1872, John M. Hyde.

3. Mary[7] Munsey, born in Gardiner, September twenty-fourth, 1852; died in Mercer, September eighth, 1854.

4. FRANK ANDREW[7] MUNSEY, born in Mercer, August twenty-first, 1854. Unmarried. Residence, New York City.

5. Delia Mary[7] Munsey, born in Bowdoin, August fifth, 1858; married Wm. Baker; died at Portland, September sixth, 1893.

6. William Cushing[7] Munsey, born in Bowdoin, October seventeenth, 1861; died Lisbon Falls, May twenty-fifth, 1873.

AUTHORITIES

Records of the Massachusetts Society of *Mayflower* Descendants. This Society admitted MR. FRANK A. MUNSEY to its membership as a lineal descendant of STEPHEN[1] and GILES[2] HOPKINS after consulting the following:

1. MUNSEY Family Record, Hopkins Family Bible.
2. History of Litchfield, Me.
3. Harpswell (Me.), Town Records.
4. Cumberland Co. (Me.), Deeds, III, 95; 66:81; 91:316 (since burned).

5. Treat Genealogy, pp. 211-262.
6. Freeman Genealogy, pp. 23-40.
7. Inscriptions, Old No. Cemetery, "Truro," p. 9.
8. *Boston Transcript,* 31 July, 1905, Cobb, Freeman.
9. *Mayflower Descendant,* Vols. I, III, and V.
10. "Who's Who in America."
11. Gravestones at Phippsburg, Me.
12. New England *Historical and Genealogical Register,* Vol. 6.
13. Maine Historical Society: Collections, 2d Series, 10:321, 322.
14. Winsor's "Duxbury."
15. Davis, "Landmarks of Plymouth."
16. "Memorial of Sprague Family."
17. Lincoln Co. (Me.) Probate Records, 100:278.
18. Georgetown (Me.) Records.
19. *Bangor Historical Magazine,* 10:137.

PART III

WHO'S WHO
IN SOME ALLIED FAMILIES

In PART III, the names of paternal (Munsey)
ancestors are printed in black, of
maternal (Hopkins) in red.

LARGE CAPITALS denote *Mayflower
passengers*; if red, they are maternal
ancestors.

SMALL CAPITALS denote other ancestors,
either paternal or maternal, on
this side the Atlantic.

47

PART III
WHO'S WHO
IN SOME ALLIED FAMILIES
(Arranged alphabetically)

THE ABORN FAMILY*
(The names of direct ancestors (other than MAYFLOWER
PASSENGERS) are in SMALL CAPITALS

The name Aborn has various spellings in the old MSS
and records (Aberne, Aberon, Abon, Aborn, Aborne,
Abourn, Abourne, Abowen, Abron, Aburn, Aburne,
Eaborn, Eaborne, Eabourn, Eabourne, Eaburn,
Eaburne, Ebborn, Ebborne, Ebern, Ebonne, Eborn,
Eborne, Eboune, Ebourn, Ebourne, Eburn, Eburne).

1. THOMAS[1] ABORNE (EBORNE) was a tanner of Salem,
   Mass. He was made a freeman 14 May 1634,
   and was still living, but very old, in 1642. Savage
   believes† his son was

2. SAMUEL[2] ABORN of Salem (1611-1700). He may
   have lived at Lynn about 1640, but he had a
   grant of land in Salem in 1639 and had several
   children baptized there in 1648. He was made a

---

*Paternal (Munsey) families are in black; maternal (Hopkins)
in red.

†Since no actual proof of this has been found, the name of
Thomas is not given on the chart.

freeman‡ in 1665. He seems to have been a free
trader; for in 1668 he was one of the signers of
a petition against imposts, addressed by certain
inhabitants of Salem to the General Court, con-
tending that customs duties would "bee an
exceeding great obstrucktion to all traffique and
Commerce which is the great staff of this Col-
lony." He married CATHERINE², daughter of
JAMES¹ SMITH, of Marblehead, who died after
1701. SAMUEL² ABORN died in 1700. He had
the following children:

1. Samuel³, born 1639±; died 1721±; married 1663/4 Susannah Trask.
2. Joseph³, living in Salem, 1704, 1708.
3. Moses³, born 1645/6, baptized at Salem, 1648.
4. MARY³, baptized at Salem 1648; married (1)—Starr;
(2) Wm. Nick of Marblehead; died before November
thirtieth, 1683; (3) 1690, DR. GEO. JACKSON; died 1722.
5. Rebecca³, baptized 1651; married 1680 Thomas Bell.
6. Hannah³, married Joseph Houlton; died 1743.
7. Sarah³, baptized 1656; married Benjamin Horn (or
Orne).

3. MARY³ ABORN was probably born in 1648, since
that was the year of her baptism. Her first husband was named Starr, her second William Nick,
of Marblehead. In 1690 she married DR. GEORGE
JACKSON, her third husband (see JACKSON
family), also of Marblehead. She died in 1722.

---

‡ In the early days of New England, before a man could vote
or hold office, he had to be made a freeman: that is, he had to
be at least 21 years of age; to be a respectable member of some
Congregational Church; to take the "Freeman's Oath" of
allegiance; and to be "admitted freeman" by the General or
Quarterly Court. After 1664, church membership was not
deemed essential, but a certificate of good character was required from some clergyman acquainted with the applicant.
This practice prevailed from 1630 to 1688.

By the marriage of Mrs. MARY³ (ABORN) [STARR-NICK] in 1690 the family of ABORN was merged in that of JACKSON, in 1736 the name of JACKSON was merged in that of PITMAN; in 1772* the name of PITMAN was merged in that of **MUNSEY.**
*Also in another line before 1749 (see PITMAN family).

AUTHORITIES

1. *Essex Antiquarian*, Vols. 1 and 2.
2. *New England Family History*, Vol. 1.
3. *N. E. Historical and Genealogical Register*, Vols. 3, 6, 8, 9, 55.
4. *"Driver Genealogy."*

THE ALDEN FAMILY†

1. JOHN¹ ALDEN, the Pilgrim, was born in England in 1599, and died in Duxbury, Mass., 12 Sept. 1687 (O. S.) in his 89th year. He married, before 1624, PRISCILLA² MULLINS (WILLIAM¹) (see MULLINS family), who died after 1650. This couple has been immortalized by the poet Longfellow, one of their lineal descendants, in his "Courtship of Miles Standish." Sent by the bluff old soldier as an envoy to the fair PRISCILLA, JOHN ALDEN presented the merits of his friend with rare unselfishness;

But as he warmed and glowed, in his simple and eloquent language,
Quite forgetful of self, and full of the praise of his rival,
Archly the maiden smiled, and, with eyes overrunning with laughter,
Said, in a tremulous voice, "Why don't you speak for yourself, John?"

---

† Maternal (Hopkins) allied families are in red; paternal (Munsey) in black.

Then he spoke—what man could have refrained?—and the wedding day was set. There were no long engagements in those days. When the time came, tradition says that JOHN ALDEN, lacking horse and carriage, brought forth a bull, spread a large piece of broadcloth on his back, mounted, and rode to the bride's house. After the ceremony he placed a cushion upon the cloth, lifted the new MRS. ALDEN— more fortunate than Europa—upon the bull's back, and led the animal home by a ring in his nose. The poet has modified the tradition but very little:

Then from a stall near at hand, amid exclamations of
    wonder,
Alden the thoughtful, the careful, so happy, so proud of
    Priscilla,
Brought out his snow-white bull, obeying the hand of its
    master,
Led by a cord that was tied to an iron ring in its nostrils,
Covered with crimson cloth, and a cushion placed for a
    saddle.
She should not walk, he said, through the dust and heat
    of the noonday;
Nay, she should ride like a queen, not plod along like a
    peasant.
Somewhat alarmed at first, but reassured by the others,
Placing her hand on the cushion, her foot in the hand of
    her husband,
Gayly, with joyous laugh, Priscilla mounted her palfrey.

JOHN ALDEN was about 21 years old when he came to America. President John Adams, a descendant, says he was the first of the Pilgrim band to spring upon

The Plymouth Rock, that had been to their feet as a
    doorstep
Into a world unknown,—the corner stone of a nation!

But we are inclined to consider this only a tradition. He was "probably the youngest of those who signed the immortal compact of civil government in the cabin of the *Mayflower*" (see BREWSTER family), and as he was the last survivor of the signers, he has fitly been styled "the personal representative of the beginning and end of the Pilgrim colonization." His entry into their ranks was unpremeditated. Bradford says of him:

> John Alden was hired for a cooper, at South-Hampton wher the ship victuled; and being a hopefull young man was much desired, but left to his owne liking to go, or stay when he came here, but he stayed and maryed here.

It may be that JOHN ALDEN joined the Pilgrims from love of adventure, and that as Goodwin suggests, in his "Pilgrim Republic," PRISCILLA MULLINS was the chief inducement for him to remain.

The rise of the young cooper was rapid in the esteem of his new found friends. "In 1627 BRADFORD, STANDISH, ALLERTON, WINSLOW, HOWLAND, ALDEN, and PRENCE agreed with the Adventurers in England to take over the whole trade of the Colony for six years, undertaking to pay all debts and arrange for the removal of the rest of the congregation from Holland." For forty-three years ALDEN was Governor's Assistant; for thirteen, Treasurer of the Colony; for eight, a member of the Council of War. He often filled several of these offices

at one time.   After 1640 we find him one of the
seven colonists styled "gentleman."

He made his home in Duxbury, eight miles
from Plymouth.   The site of his well is still
shown, near the "Old Alden House," which was
built by his grandson, Col. John Alden.   As late
as 1901, an Alden had always occupied the house.
JOHN ALDEN'S Bible may be seen in Pilgrim Hall, Plymouth.   His autographs are rare.
One of them was owned by the late Henry D.
Forbes, of Boston, appended to a deed given on
January 8, 1679/80, but never recorded.   A pho-
tographic reproduction of this deed is in the
seventh volume of the "*Mayflower Descendant.*"
Another autograph may be seen at the Boston
Public Library, at the close of a letter written
by Gov. BRADFORD to Gov. Winthrop in 1631.
The letter, a kind of state document, is signed
not only by the writer, but by several other
prominent men of the colony, including JOHN
ALDEN and Thomas Prence.

There are in existence two broadsides of dog-
gerel rhyme, one of 66 lines, another of 100,
printed on the occasion of JOHN ALDEN'S
death.   A reproduction of each is in the ninth
volume of the "*Mayflower Descendant.*"   The
first is full of pious hyperbole, and compares the
Pilgrim with numerous Patriarchs of note, yet
never to his disadvantage.   The other broadside
is in the archives of the Boston Athenaeum.   It
is signed with the initials "J. C.", which are supposed to indicate John Cotton.   The poetry is

indifferent, but there are no parallels so startling as in the first case. The author concludes the poem with some rhymes about a curious anagram made out of the letters of the name IOHN ALDEN, viz.:

END AL ON HI'

JOHN¹ ALDEN and PRISCILLA² MULLINS had eleven children:

1. ELIZABETH² ALDEN, born 1623±; married 1644 WILLIAM¹ PAYBODY; died 1717.
2. John₂ Alden, born 1626±; married (1) Elizabeth ——(?) (2) Mrs. Elizabeth Phillips, widow of Abiel Everell; died 1702.
3. Joseph² Alden, born 1627; married Mary Simmons; died 1697.
4. Sarah² Alden, born 1629; married Alexander² Standish (Miles¹); died 1688±.
5. Jonathan² Alden, born 1632±; married Abigail Hallet; died 1697.
6. Ruth² Alden, born 16—; married John Bass; died 1674. She was ancestress of John Adams and John Quincy Adams.
7. Mary² Alden, born 16—; married Thomas Delano, or De la Noye, of Duxbury; died 1699±.
8. David² Alden, born 1646; married Mary Southworth; died 1719.
9. Priscilla² Alden, married Samuel Cheeseborough.
10. Rebecca² Alden, of marriageable age in 1661.
11. Zachariah² Alden, said to be ancestor of William Cullen Bryant.

2. ELIZABETH² ALDEN (JOHN¹) was born in 1623 or 1624; on December twenty-sixth, 1644, she married WILLIAM¹ PAYBODY, of Duxbury (see PEABODY family). She died in Little Compton, R. I., June seventeenth, 1717. In the *Boston*

News Letter of that date, there appeared the following:

This morning died here [at Little Compton], ELIZABETH PAYBODY, in the 93d year of her age. She was a daughter of JOHN ALDEN, ESQ., and PRISCILLA, his wife, daughter of MR. WILLIAM MULLINS This JOHN ALDEN and PRISCILLA MULLINS were married at Plymouth, where their daughter ELIZABETH was born. She was exemplary, virtuous, and pious, and her memory is blessed. Her granddaughter Bradford is a grandmother.

By the marriage of ELIZABETH² ALDEN in 1644
the name of ALDEN was merged in that of PAYBODY; in 1683
the name of PAYBODY was merged in that of BARTLETT; in 1738
the name of BARTLETT was merged in that of SPRAGUE; in 1812
the name of SPRAGUE was merged in that of HOPKINS, in 1847
the name of HOPKINS was merged in that of MUNSEY.

THE ANDREWS FAMILY

1. HENRY¹ ANDREWS, of Taunton, Mass., was included in the list of freemen from Cohannet, dated March seventh, 1636. He was one of the purchasers of Taunton in 1637. He was one of the deputies in 1639, when the town was first organized, and also in 1643, 1644, 1647, and 1649. He built the first meeting-house in Taunton, in payment for which, in whole or in part, the town conveyed to him, in 1647, the "Calf Pasture." He died in 1652. The maiden name of his wife MARY is unknown. He had the following children:

   1. Henry² Andrews, married Mary Wadsworth; killed by Indians in 1676.
   2. Mary² Andrews, married (1) William Hodges; (2) Peter Pitts.

3. ABIGAIL² ANDREWS, born 1647; married, 1667, DEACON JOHN² WADSWORTH; died 1723.
4. Sarah² Andrews, married, 1664, Jared Talbut.

2. ABIGAIL² ANDREWS (HENRY¹) was born in Taunton, Mass., in 1647. On July twenty-fifth, 1667, she married DEACON JOHN² W A D S W O R T H (CHRISTOPHER¹), of Duxbury. (See WADSWORTH family). She died "about Midnight betwixt ye 24th and 25th" of November, 1723.

By the marriage of ABIGAIL² ANDREWS in 1667
the name of ANDREWS was merged in that of WADSWORTH; in ——
the name of WADSWORTH was merged in that of SPRAGUE; in 1812
the name of SPRAGUE was merged in that of HOPKINS, in 1847
the name of HOPKINS was merged in that of **MUNSEY.**

AUTHORITIES

1. "Henry Andrews, of Taunton." Drummond.
2. *Mayflower Descendant*, Vols. 9 and 11.
3. "Two hundred and Fifty Years of the Wadsworth Family in America." Wadsworth.
4. "History of the Andrews Family."
5. "Origin and History of the Name of Andrews."

THE BANGS FAMILY

1. EDWARD¹ BANGS was born about 1592 at Chichester, or Chester, England, and came to Plymouth Colony in 1623, in the ship *Ann*. He married after 1627 Lydia² Hicks, daughter of Robert¹ and Margaret Hicks, by whom he had a son, John² Bangs. Lydia died before 1637, and Edward married REBECCA——, who became the mother of nine children. EDWARD¹ BANGS moved with GOVERNOR PRINCE to Eastham in 1644, and settled near where the Pilgrims first set foot on land, previous to landing on Plymouth Rock. He was a Pilgrim also; for that title is bestowed on all who came over in the first three ships to Plymouth, viz., the *Mayflower* (1620), the *Fortune* (1621), and the *Ann* (1623). He was made a freeman in 1633. He filled many offices of trust, both at Plymouth and Eastham; thus, he was Assessor, Selectman, Town Treasurer, Deputy to the Colony Court, Overseer of the guard against the Indians, etc., etc. Before going to Eastham he superintended, as shipwright, the building of the "first ship of size," launched at Plymouth, a bark of forty or fifty tons, costing about two hundred pounds. On condition of his contributing one-sixteenth of the expense, the town granted him eighty acres of land. In 1657 we find him a merchant in Eastham. He died there in 1677/8.

His children were as follows:

By Lydia Hicks:

1. John[2] Bangs; married, 1660, Hannah Smalley.

By REBECCA ——

2. Lieut. Joshua[2] Bangs; born, 1637; married, 1669, Hannah Scudder; died, 1709.
3. Rebecca[2] Bangs; married, 1654, Capt. Jonathan Sparrow (first wife); died before 1677.
4. Sarah[2] Bangs; married, 1656, Capt. Thomas Howes; died, 1683.
5. Capt. Jonathan[2] Bangs; born, 1640; married (1), 1664, Mary[3] Mayo (Samuel[2], Rev. John[1]); (2) Sarah ——; (3) 1720, Mrs. Ruth Young.
6. LYDIA[2] BANGS, born, 1642±; married, (1) 1661, BENJAMIN[2] HIGGINS (see HIGGINS family); (2) Nicholas Snow; died, 1709+.

7. Hannah² Bangs; married, 1662, John Doane.
8. Bethia² Bangs; born 1650, married Gershom Hall.
9. Apphia² Bangs; born 1651; married (1) December twenty-eighth, 1670, John Knowles; (2) Stephen Atwood.
10. Mercy² Bangs (twin with Apphia); born 1651; married, December twenty-eighth, 1670, Stephen Merrick.

2. LYDIA² BANGS (EDWARD¹) was born in Eastham, Mass., about 1642. Her first husband was BENJAMIN² HIGGINS (RICHARD¹) (see HIGGINS family), whom she married December twenty-fourth, 1661. She had nine children by this marriage, the last of whom was born in 1681. In 1691 her husband died, and she subsequently married Nicholas Snow. She was living at Eastham in 1709.

By the marriage of LYDIA² BANGS in 1661
the name of BANGS was merged in that of HIGGINS, subsequently
the name of HIGGINS was merged in that of PEPPER, in 1754
the name of PEPPER was merged in that of MEREEN, in 1748
the name of MEREEN was merged in that of HOPKINS; and in 1847
the name of HOPKINS was merged in that of **MUNSEY.**

AUTHORITIES

1. "The Bangs Family." Dudley.
2. *Mayflower Descendant*, Vols. 1, 4, 5, 6, 7, 8, 11, 12, 14.
3. *N. E. Historical and Genealogical Register*, Vols. 6, 8, 9, 10, 22, 23, 27.
4. *New England Family History*, Vol. 2.

THE BARTLETT FAMILY

1. ROBERT¹ BARTLETT, the pioneer Bartlett of New England, came to Plymouth in the ship *Ann*, in July, 1623. He married, about 1629, MARY, daughter of RICHARD¹ and ELIZABETH

WARREN. Richard came over in the *Mayflower*, in 1620; his wife and children were fellow passengers with young Bartlett, two years later (see WARREN family).

ROBERT[1] BARTLETT was a cooper by trade. The records show that he was a man of good standing in the community, and highly respected by his associates. He lived and died in Manomet, Plymouth, where his possessions were. He passed away in 1676, aged 73. His wife outlived him, but died between 1677 and 1683. His homestead has been known as the "Bartlett farm," and has been in the possession of the BARTLETT family continuously up to the present. The house, built in 1680, is still standing.

ROBERT[1] and MARY (WARREN) BARTLETT, had eight children:—

1. Rebecca[2] Bartlett, born perhaps 1630; married, 1649 (as his first wife), William Harlow; died between June second, 1657, and July fifteenth, 1658.
2. Mary[2] Bartlett, born perhaps 1631 or 1632; married (1) 1651, Richard Foster; (2) 1659 (as his first wife), Jonathan Morey.
3. BENJAMIN[2] BARTLETT, born before June sixth, 1633; married (1) Susanna Jenney; (2) 1656, SARAH[4] BREWSTER (LOVE[2], WILLIAM[1]); (3) Cecilia ——; died, 1691.
4. Sarah[2] Bartlett, born perhaps 1635; married, 1656, Samuel[2] Rider (Samuel[1]); died before 1680.
5. Joseph[2] Bartlett, born 1638; died 1711. Was ancestor of Longfellow in the following line: Joseph[2], Joseph[3], Samuel[4], Elizabeth[5] (who married Gen. Peleg[5] Wadsworth), Zilpah[6] Wadsworth (married Stephen[5] Longfellow), *Henry Wadsworth Longfellow*. Another genealogist gives Longfellow's descent thus: Benjamin[2], Benjamin[3], Priscilla[4] Bartlett, Susanna Sampson,

Peleg Wadsworth, Zilpah Wadsworth, *Henry Wadsworth Longfellow.*

6. Elizabeth[2] Bartlett, born perhaps 1640; married, 1661/2, Anthony Sprague of Hingham; died in 1712.
7. Lydia[2] Bartlett, born 1648; married (1) James Barnaby, who was living in 1712; (2) John Nelson.
8. Mercy[2] Bartlett, born 1650/1; married, 1668/9, John Ivey of Boston.

2. BENJAMIN[2] BARTLETT (ROBERT[1]), whose father married MARY[2] WARREN (RICHARD[1]), was born in Plymouth. Since he was made a freeman on June sixth, 1654, he must have been born before June sixth, 1633. He was three times married. His first wife was Susanna[2], daughter of John[1] and Sarah (Carey) Jenney; his second wife was SARAH[3] BREWSTER (LOVE[2], WILLIAM[1]), whom he married in 1656 (see BREWSTER family); in 1678 he had a third wife, Cecilia ——, whose maiden name has not been discovered. She outlived her husband but a short time.

BENJAMIN[2] BARTLETT settled in Duxbury, where he became one of the most prominent citizens. He was chosen constable in 1662. "This was an office of high trust and responsibility, and none were elected to it but men of good standing." In 1666-7 CHRISTOPHER[1] WADSWORTH, Josiah Standish, and BENJAMIN[2] BARTLETT were the selectmen of Duxbury. For 18 years BENJAMIN[2] BARTLETT was on the Board, and in 1690-91 was chairman. He was Representative to the General Court in 1685. He died during the week beginning August 21, 1691, leaving a farm valued at one hundred forty pounds and

other property amounting to two hundred fifty
pounds.   He left, by his second wife, six children,
four sons and two daughters:—

1. Benjamin³ Bartlett, born perhaps 1657; married, 1676
   or 1678, Ruth Paybody.
2. SAMUEL³ BARTLETT, married, 1683, HANNAH² PAYBODY
   (WILLIAM¹); died 1713.
3. Ichabod³ Bartlett, married (1) 1699, Elizabeth Waterman of Marshfield, Mass.; (2) 1709, Desire Arnold
   of Duxbury.
4. Ebenezer³ Bartlett, born Duxbury; married Hannah
   ——; died before 1712.
5. Rebecca³ Bartlett, married, 1679, Wm. Bradford.
6. Sarah³ Bartlett, married, 1687, Robert Bartlett.

3. SAMUEL³ BARTLETT (BENJAMIN², ROBERT¹) was
   a "mariner" of Duxbury, but died or removed
   before 1713.   On August second, 1683, he married
   HANNAH² PAYBODY (WILLIAM¹) (see PEABODY
   family), by whom he had the following children:—

1. Benjamin⁴ Bartlett, born 1684; married, 1702, Sarah
   Barnes.
2. JOSEPH⁴ BARTLETT, born 1686; married, 1714, LYDIA⁴
   NELSON.
3. Samuel⁴ Bartlett, born 1691; an officer at Louisburg;
   ancestor of the author of "Familiar Quotations,"
   John⁸ Bartlett.
4. Ichabod⁴ Bartlett, born perhaps 1693; married, 1721,
   Susanna Spooner.
5. Judah⁴ Bartlett.
6. William⁴ Bartlett, of Duxbury; perhaps married, 1716,
   Sarah Foster of Plymouth.
   Perhaps, also,
7. Hannah⁴ Bartlett, who married, 1714, Benjamin Arnold.

4. JOSEPH⁴ BARTLETT (SAMUEL³, BENJAMIN², RO-
   BERT¹) was born April 22, 1686, in Duxbury,
   Mass.   On December ninth, 1714, he married

Lydia[3] Nelson (John[2], William[1]) of Plymouth. She was born in 1694 and died in 1739. He died January ninth, 1764. Their children were:—

1. Isaiah[5] Bartlett, born 1715/6.
2. Patience[5] Bartlett, born 1718; married, 1738, Jethro[4] Sprague.
3. Hannah[5] Bartlett, born 1721; died 1739.
4. Lydia[5] Bartlett, born 1725; married, 1740, Bezaleel Alden.
5. Benjamin[5] Bartlett, born 1730/1.
6. Sarah[5] Bartlett, born 1732.
7. Bathsheba[5] Bartlett, born 1738.

5. Patience[5] Bartlett (Joseph[4], Samuel[3], Benjamin[2], Robert[1]) was born in Duxbury, Mass., on July twenty-seventh, 1718. On "December ye 12th, 1738 Jethro Sprague [see Sprague family] & Patience Bartlit both of Duxborough were Joyned together in Marriage, pr Edward Arnold Justice of ye Peace."* She died in 1741.

By the marriage of Patience[5] Bartlett, in 1738,
the name of Bartlett was merged in that of Sprague, in 1812
the name of Sprague was merged in that of HOPKINS, in 1847
the name of HOPKINS was merged in that of MUNSEY.

---

*The legal celebration of marriage was by a civil magistrate only, in the earlier years of New England history. The reason was, that the Church of Rome had exalted marriage to the rank of a sacrament; against this the Puritans protested, and treated marriage purely as a civil contract. But after a time this extreme theory was abandoned, and by the end of the 17th Century we find pastors performing the marriage service. The earliest record in Massachusetts of a marriage by a minister, is 1686. See E. H. Byington's *The Puritan in England and New England*, p. 165. Cf. *Watertown Records*, p. 96.

AUTHORITIES

1. "Lawrence and Bartlett Memorials."
2. *Mayflower Descendant*, Vols. 1, 2, *3*, *6*, 8, 9, 11, 12, 13, *14*.
3. *Massachusetts Magazine*, Vol. 2.
4. "Sketches of the Bartlett Family."

THE BASSETT FAMILY

1. WILLIAM[1] BASSETT was the first of his family to set foot on American soil. He lived in Plymouth, or Sandwich, England, whence he went to Leyden, Holland, in quest of religious liberty. In 1621, he came to this country in the ship *Fortune*, landing at Plymouth, Massachusetts, in November.

In the first distribution of land among the Pilgrims in 1623, WILLIAM[1] BASSETT received two acres, but no mention was then made of his wife or family. In the allotment of cattle, in 1627, we find mention of a wife, ELIZABETH, and two children, William and Elizabeth. It has been said that he married an Elizabeth Tilden. But there seems to have been no Elizabeth Tilden in the colony at that time, so far as can be proved. At present we must insist that the maiden name of ELIZABETH BASSETT remains undiscovered. Whoever she may have been, she died previously to her husband; for two wills, one by Timothy Hatherly in 1664 and a second by WILLIAM[1] BASSETT himself, made in 1667, taken with the inventory of his property, show that a wife, Mary Bassett, outlived WILLIAM[1].

According to the belief of some, WILLIAM[1]

BASSETT had four wives and narrowly escaped a
fifth.   There are foreign records which prove con-
clusively that in 1611 a William Bassett of Sandwich, England, a widower of Cecilia Leight, was
affianced to Margaret Butler on the 19th of
March.   She died before the third reading of the
banns, however, and on the 13th of August
William consoled himself with another Margaret at Leyden, whose maiden name was Oldham.
Was this the same WILLIAM as the husband of
ELIZABETH and Mary?

One of the descendants of WILLIAM and
. ELIZABETH, Mr. Abbott Bassett, at one time
President of the Bassett Family Association, with
much reason argues as follows:

"'The man of Leyden was not a young man.
The *Mayflower* brought over 'the youngest and
the strongest of the Pilgrims.' WILLIAM BASSETT
was neither young nor strong, since he came not
on the *Mayflower*.   Those who have examined
the record carefully claim that it is impossible
that it was the husband of Margaret Oldham
who came to America, married twice on this side
of the water, and became the father of six children.   We have yet to find who it was that came
in the *Fortune*."

But whether WILLIAM BASSETT sailed from
Leyden or from Plymouth, whether he was the
husband of four wives or two, he played no small
part in the activities of the Plymouth Colony.
His name is on the earliest list of freemen, in
1633.   In private life he was an armourer and

blacksmith. He was a volunteer in the company raised in 1637 to aid Massachusetts and Connecticut in the Pequot War. He was a member of the commission that laid out the bounds of Duxbury, and for six years was Representative to the Old Colony Court. Everything shows him to have been a highly respected member of the commonwealth.

He lived in Plymouth seventeen years, his home being about four hundred feet north of where the Samoset House now stands. About 1638 he moved to Duxbury, where in 1640 his name was among the highest on the tax list. In 1652 he became one of the founders of Bridgewater and one of the largest landowners there.

He was a man of liberal culture, and at his death owned a larger library than any other of the colonists. Many of his descendants have been illustrious. One married a sister of Martha Washington, and was a member of Congress from 1805 to 1830; another, Richard Bassett, signed the Constitution of the United States; while Elizabeth Bassett, the wife of Benjamin Harrison, a signer of the Declaration of Independence, was mother of one of our Presidents and great-grandmother of another.

WILLIAM¹ BASSETT died at Bridgewater in 1667, leaving six or seven children, all by his wife Elizabeth:—

1. William² Bassett, born 1624; died 1670. It is in dispute whether this is the William Bassett who married Mary Burt of Lynn.

2. Elizabeth[2] Bassett, born 1626; married, 1648, Thomas Burgess, Jr.
3. Nathaniel[2] Bassett, born 1628; married Dorcas (or Mary) Joyce.
4. Joseph[2] Bassett, born 1629; married, 1677, Martha Hobart
5. Sarah[2] Bassett, born 1630; married, 1648, Lieutenant PEREGRINE WHITE, who was born ON THE *MAYFLOWER* in Cape Cod Harbor, before the Pilgrims landed.
6. RUTH[2] BASSETT, born 1632; married,[1] 1655, JOHN[2] SPRAGUE, and perhaps another, after SPRAGUE's death.

probably also

7. Jane[2] Bassett, born 1634; married Thomas Gilbert.

2. RUTH[2] BASSETT (WILLIAM[1]) was born in Duxbury, Mass., in 1632. In 1655 she married a fellow townsman, JOHN[2] SPRAGUE (FRANCIS[1]) by whom she had three sons and four daughters. Her husband (see SPRAGUE family) was killed by the Indians in 1676, and the widow is said to have married —— Thomas.

By the marriage of RUTH[2] BASSETT, in 1655,
    the name of BASSETT was merged in that of SPRAGUE, in 1812
    the name of SPRAGUE was merged in that of HOPKINS,
    and in 1847
    the name of HOPKINS was merged in that of MUNSEY.

AUTHORITIES
1. "England and Holland of the Pilgrims." Dexter.
2. "The Bassett Family."
3. "Bassett Family Association Reunions."
4. *Transcript* Clippings (Index and Scrap Book at Public Library of Lynn, Mass.)

THE BATE(S) FAMILY

1. CLEMENT[1] BATE, of Biddenden, Kent, England, with his wife, ANN(E), and five children,—James, Clement, Jr., Rachel, Joseph, and Benjamin,—are on the passenger list of the *Planter*, which

sailed from London to America April sixth,
1635; but something seems to have delayed
them, for they came over in the *Elizabeth,*
which sailed on the 13th of the same month.
With this family came James Bate, a brother
of CLEMENT[1], who settled in Dorchester. CLEM-
ENT[1] went to Hingham, and became one of its
prominent citizens. At various times the town
granted him about forty acres of land, in lots va-
rying in size from one acre to twenty. He was
a tailor by trade. The records show that he
was chosen one of the first three Selectmen of
the town of Hingham, March twenty-third,
1637; and that subsequently he was often chosen by his fellow townsmen to offices of trust
requiring tact and judgment. He died at Hingham September seventeenth, 1671. He lived on
South Street. His wife died October first, 1669.

The ancestors of CLEMENT[1] BATE lived for
several generations in Lydd, England. His
father, [1]James, died there in 1614; he was the son
of [2]John, who died in 1580; his father, [3]Andrew,
died in 1533; his father, [4]John, died in 1522; his
father was either [5]James or [5]Thomas, the latter
of whom died in 1485; both [5]James and [5]Thomas
are mentioned in the will of [6]Henry, probably
their father, who died in 1478.

CLEMENT[1] BATE was baptized January twenty-
second, 1594/5 at Lydd. Later he moved to
Biddenden, Kent Co. His wife's name was
ANN(E), but the date and place of his marriage

are still unknown, and also his wife's maiden name. Their children were as follows:—

1. James[2] Bate, born 1621±; married, 1643, Ruth Lyford; died 1689.
2. Clement[2] Bate, born 1623±; drowned November, 1639.
3. John[2] Bate, baptized October eighteenth, 1624; died December eighteenth, same year.
4. Rachel[2] Bate, baptized October twenty-second, 1626; died 1647.
5. JOSEPH[2] BATE, baptized September twenty-eighth, 1628; married, 1658, ESTHER[2] HILLIARD; died 1706.
6. Child buried unbaptized April second, 1631.
7. Lieutenant Benjamin[2] Bate, baptized June twenty-fourth, 1632; died 1678; married Jane (Weeks?).

The above were born in England.

8. Samuel[2] Bate, baptized in Hingham, March twenty-fourth, 1639; married, 1667, Lydia Lapham of Scituate.
9. Hopestill[2] Bate, born at Hingham; baptized September, 1644; died following December.

2. JOSEPH[2] BATE (CLEMENT[1]) was baptized at All Saints Church, Biddenden, Kent, England, September twenty-eighth, 1628. He came with his father and their family to Hingham, Massachusetts, in 1635. He married in Hingham, January ninth, 1657/8 ESTHER[2], daughter of WILLIAM[1] HILLIARD. She was born in 1642 and died June third, 1709. JOSEPH[2] BATE died April thirtieth, 1706, "aged 76."* In his will of April twenty-fourth, 1706, he mentions and names his wife and four sons, and mentions but does not name his four daughters. He was a bricklayer, constable from 1675 to 1678; selectman 1671, 1677,

---

* So says the record: but there is obviously an error in the computation, since he was born in 1628.

1684, and 1692; sexton of the parish from 1673 for many years. His children, all born at Hingham:—

1. Joseph[3] Bate, born September twenty-eighth, 1660.
2. Esther[3] Bate, born August twenty-ninth, 1663; married in Boston, September sixteenth, 1691, Richard[2] Cobb.
3. Caleb[3] Bate, born March thirtieth, 1666.
4. Hannah[3] Bate, born October thirty-first, 1668.
5. Joshua[3] Bate, born August fourteenth, 1671; married Rachel Tower.
6. Bathsheba[3] Bate, born January twenty-sixth, 1673/4.
7. Clement[3] Bate, born September twenty-second, 1676; drowned June twenty-ninth, 1706.
8. Eleanor[3] Bate, born August twenty-ninth, 1679; died September eighth following.
9. Abigail[3] Bate, born October sixteenth, 1680; married June twelfth, 1704, John Chubbuck.

From Joseph[2] Bate, of Hingham, was descended Hon. John Lewis Bates of Boston, Ex-Governor of Massachusetts, in the following line:

Joseph[2] Bates married Esther[2] Hilliard; their son
Joshua[3] Bates   married Rachel Tower; their son
Joshua[4] Bates   married Abigail Joy; their son
Joshua[5] Bates   married (1) Grace Lincoln; their son
Levi[6] Bates   married (1) Hannah Litchfield; their son
Lewis[7] Bates   married Elizabeth Webster; their son
Lewis Benton[8] Bates married Louisa Derry Field; their son was
Governor John Lewis[9] Bates.

3. Esther[3] Bate (Joseph[2], Clement[1]) of Hingham was born on August twenty-ninth, 1663; she was married in Boston, September sixteenth, 1691, "by Samuel Sewall, Esq.*, Assist.," to Richard[2], son of Thomas[1] Cobb, then living in Boston (see Cobb family).

*See footnote on page 63.

By the marriage of ESTHER[3] BATE, in 1691,
the name of BATE was merged in that of COBB, in 1755
the name of COBB was merged in that of HOPKINS, in 1847
the name of HOPKINS was merged in that of **MUNSEY**.

AUTHORITIES

1. *N.E. Historical and Genealogical Register*, Vols. 2 and 66.
2. Waters's "Gleanings," Vol. 2.
3. Savage's "Genealogical Dictionary."
4. Lincoln's "Hingham."
5. 9th "Report" of the Record Commissioners of Boston.
6. "The Bates Family of Cummington."
7. "The Bates Bulletin."
8. MS. of Isaac C. Bates, in Boston Historic-Genealogical Library.
9. Hingham Records.

THE BRAY FAMILY

1. JOHN[1] BRAY came to Piscataqua from Plymouth, England about 1660. He brought with him his wife JOAN, and a daughter MARGERY[2] one year old. He settled at Kittery, Maine, as shipwright; in 1674 he also kept an inn. Savage says he "removed in the war [King Philip's] to Gloucester, perhaps; there married November tenth, 1679, Margaret Lambert, as second wife." It is not known when or where his first wife died. He himself died in 1690.

The house of JOHN[1] BRAY at Kittery is still standing. Edward Whitefield, in "Homes of our Forefathers," says:—"This is a very fine old house, built by John Bray in 1660." Referring to a rude oil painting of the siege of Louisburg, which is on a panel over the parlor fireplace, he says:—

2. "Margery² Bray (John¹), married Colonel William¹ Pepperrell in 1678 (see Pepperrell family), and became the mother of Sir William²
Pepperrell, of Louisburg fame, [and of Joanna²,
an ancestress of the Munseys]. The Bray
house, considered old even then, was occupied
at the time of Sir William's famous campaign†
by Capt. Deering, his cousin, also a grandson
of the old shipbuilder. As he served in front
of Louisburg, this rough sketch was no doubt
the work of his own hand." Thus it would
seem that John¹ Bray had another daughter,
who married a Deering. Margery² (Bray)
Pepperrell died April twenty-fourth, 1741.
Her historian speaks of her as "exemplary for
unaffected piety and amiable virtue, especially
her charity, her courteous affability, her prudence, meekness, patience, and unweariedness in
well-doing."

By the marriage of Margery² Bray, in 1678,
the name of Bray was merged in that of Pepperrell; in 1711
the name of Pepperrell was merged in that of Jackson; in 1736
the name of Jackson was merged in that of Pitman; in 1772*
the name of Pitman was merged in that of **MUNSEY**.

AUTHORITIES
1. *New England Family History*, Vol. 1.
2. Savage's "Genealogical Dictionary."
3. "Homes of our Forefathers." *Whitefield*. Vol. 4.
4. *New England Magazine*.
5. Brunswick (Me.) *Telegraph*, September sixteenth,
   1870.
6. "The Driver Family."

† See page 142.
* As also before 1749, in another line (see Pitman family).

THE BREWSTER FAMILY

1. ELDER WILLIAM[1] BREWSTER was a ruling
elder of the Plymouth Church which founded
Plymouth Colony in 1620. He was born in the
latter part of 1566, or early in 1567, probably at
Scrooby, Nottinghamshire, England. He was
the son of William and Prudence Brewster, of
Scrooby. His father died in 1590. For many
years he had been receiver of Scrooby, and
bailiff of the manor house; he also had held
the office of "Post," which had in turn been
held by *his* father, the grandfather of ELDER
WILLIAM. On December third, 1580, at the
early age of fourteen, ELDER WILLIAM[1]
matriculated at Peterhouse, one of the colleges
forming the University of Cambridge, England;
but he does not appear to have remained long
enough to receive a degree. He was next appointed assistant clerk to William Davison, Secretary of State to Queen Elizabeth; accompanied
that gentleman on his embassy to the Nether-
lands, in August, 1585; and served him at court
until his downfall in 1587. ELDER WILLIAM[1]
then returned to the manor house at Scrooby,
and three years later was administrator of his
father's estate. He was soon appointed "Post,"
and held that office till September thirtieth,
1607.

At an early age he became a convert to the
doctrine of John Robinson, the founder of Con-
gregationalism; after his return to Scrooby, his

residence, the manor house, became the place of worship on the Lord's Day for all members of the new church in that vicinity. There BREW-STER "with great love entertained them when they came, making prouission for them to his great charge."

At length the government began to enforce the strict laws against the new religion, on which account, in 1607, ELDER WILLIAM[1] and his fellow members determined to flee to Holland. He, with several others, was arrested at Boston, England, and detained for several weeks; but he finally made his way to Leyden, the rendezvous of the new church. Here he resided for about twelve years, during which time he was engaged in teaching and printing. Finally it became necessary to secure a new home for the growing church, and it was decided that a part of the members should emigrate to America.

"So they left that goodly and pleasant city which had been their resting place for near twelve years; but they knew that they were PILGRIMS, and looked not much on those things, but lifted up their eyes to the heavens, their dearest country, and quieted their spirits."

BREWSTER, whom we have called "Elder" by anticipation, was Elder now in fact, and was chosen to lead the first party. Accordingly he, his wife MARY, and their two sons LOVE[2] and WRESTLING[2] embarked in the *Mayflower*, which sailed from Plymouth, England, on September sixteenth, 1620, and dropped anchor in Plymouth Harbor, Massachusetts, on the twenty-sixth of December. The historic landing on Plymouth Rock had been made five days earlier.

A great mistake was made in sending out the colony at that season of the year. The first awful winter which the Pilgrims endured *halved* their number. At one time there were but seven well persons, of whom one was ELDER BREWSTER. BRADFORD says these seven tended the sick, washed their loathsome linen, and performed duties "which dainty and queazy stomachs cannot endure to hear named. And yet the Lord so upheld these persons that they were not at all infected."

In a true sense ELDER BREWSTER was what his biographer Steele entitled him, the "Chief of the Pilgrims." In view of what one of his descendants has said, we may not inaptly style him the Moses of the English Exodus; for he certainly chose to suffer affliction with the people of God rather than live at ease in royal favor. But if BREWSTER was Chief, why was he not, like BRADFORD, WINSLOW, and PRINCE, made Governor of Plymouth Colony? The historian Hutchinson explains this when he says:

He was their ruling Elder, which seems to have been the bar to his being their Governor—civil and ecclesiastical office, in the same person, being then deemed incompatible.

ELDER BREWSTER was by far the most learned man among the early colonists; at his death he left a library of four hundred volumes,

sixty-two of which were in Latin. For thirty
years he preached to the Pilgrims, but there is no
indication that he ever received a dollar for his
services. GOV. BRADFORD says:

He taught twice every Sabbath, and that both power-
fully and profitably, to the great contentment of his
hearers, and their comfortable edification; yea, many
were brought to God by his ministrie. He did more in
this behalf in a year, than many that have their hundreds
a year do in their lives.

There is little doubt that BREWSTER was
the author of the famous Compact, drawn up in
the cabin of the *Mayflower* on November twenty-
first, 1620,—"the first Declaration of Independence in America, albeit with loyalty to the
king." It has been justly styled the "germ of
all our American Constitutions." It runs as
follows:—

In yᵉ name of God Amen. We whose names are under-
writen, the loyall subjects of our dread soveraigne lord
King James, by yᵉ grace of God, of great Britaine, Franc,
& Ireland king, defender of yᵉ faith, &c.
Haveing undertaken, for yᵉ glorie of God, and advance-
mente of yᵉ christian faith and honour of our king &
countrie, a voyage to plant yᵉ first colonie in yᵉ Northerne
parts of Virginia. Doe by these presents solemnly & mu-
tualy in yᵉ presence of God, and one of another; covenant, & combine our selves togeather into a civill body
politick; for our better ordering, & preservation & further-
ance of yᵉ ends aforesaid; and by vertue hearof to enacte,
constitute, and frame shuch just & equall lawes, ordi-
nances, Acts., constitutions, & offices, from time to time,
as shall be thought most meete and convenient for yᵉ
generall good of yᵉ Colonie: unto which we promise all
due submission and obedience. In witnes wherof we
have hereunder subscribed our names at Cape-Codd yᵉ
.11. of November, in yᵉ year of yᵉ raigne of our soveraigne
lord King James of England, France, & Ireland yᵉ eighteenth, and of Scotland yᵉ fiftie fourth. Anᵒ: Dom. 1620.

Forty-one Pilgrims signed the foregoing compact, among whom were:

WILLIAM BREWSTER
JOHN ALDEN
WILLIAM MULLINS
RICHARD WARREN
STEPHEN HOPKINS.

The maiden name of MARY BREWSTER is not known. She seems to have married ELDER BREWSTER soon after he returned from Queen Elizabeth's court to Scrooby. She died on April seventeenth, 1627, but her husband lived until April tenth, 1644. The children of ELDER WILLIAM[1] and MARY BREWSTER were:

1. Jonathan[2] Brewster, born 1593, at Scrooby; came to Plymouth in 1621; married, 1624, Lucretia Oldham.
2. PATIENCE[2] BREWSTER, married, 1624, GOVERNOR THOMAS PRENCE.
3. Fear[2] Brewster, married, 1626, Isaac Allerton.
4. A child[2], died at Leyden in 1609.
5. LOVE[2] BREWSTER, came in the *Mayflower;* married, in 1635, SARAH[2], daughter of WILLIAM[1] COLLIER.
6. WRESTLING[2] BREWSTER, came in the *Mayflower;* died unmarried between 1627 and 1644.

2. 1. PATIENCE[2] BREWSTER (WILLIAM[1]) came to America in the ship *Ann*, in July, 1623. On August fifth, 1624, she became the first wife of THOMAS[1] PRENCE, of Plymouth (see PRINCE family).

By the marriage of PATIENCE[2] BREWSTER, in 1624,
  the name of BREWSTER was merged in that of PRENCE,
  in 1649/50
  the name of PRENCE was merged in that of FREEMAN I; in 1717
  the name of FREEMAN I was merged in that of COBB, in 1755
  the name of COBB was merged in that of HOPKINS, in 1847
  the name of HOPKINS was merged in that of MUNSEY in
  the ninth generation; but in another line the name BREWSTER
  was continued for another generation (the tenth), as follows:

2. 2. LOVE[2] BREWSTER (WILLIAM[1]) came over
in the *Mayflower* in 1620, with his parents
WILLIAM[1] and MARY BREWSTER, and his
brother WRESTLING[2]. He married at Plymouth, on May fifteenth, 1634 (O. S.), SARAH[2],
daughter of WILLIAM[1] COLLIER (see COLLIER
family). He died at Duxbury in 1651. In 1656
his widow married Richard Parke, of Cambridge,
Massachusetts. She outlived her second husband, returned to Plymouth, and there died in
1691. LOVE[2] BREWSTER removed early
from Plymouth to Duxbury and devoted himself
to farming. In 1637 his name appears among
the volunteers in the Pequot War. He was also
a member of Capt. Miles Standish's Duxbury
Company in 1643. In the last named year he
was a grand juryman from Duxbury, and in 1645
one of the proprietors of the extension of Duxbury, now Bridgewater. His will, dated October
sixth, 1650 (O. S.) is recorded among the Plymouth Colony Wills. His estate was appraised
at ninety-seven pounds, seven shillings, one
penny.

The children of LOVE[2] and SARAH[2] (COLLIER) BREWSTER were:

1. SARAH[3] BREWSTER married, about 1656, BENJAMIN[2] BARTLETT.
2. Nathaniel[3] Brewster, married Sarah——; died 1676.
3. William[3] Brewster.
4. Wrestling[3] Brewster.

3. SARAH[3] BREWSTER (LOVE[2], WILLIAM[1]) was the second wife of BENJAMIN[2] BARTLETT (ROBERT[1]) of Duxbury, whom she married as his second wife about 1656 (see BARTLETT family). SARAH[3] (BREWSTER) BARTLETT was the direct ancestress of the poet Longfellow through her eldest son, Benjamin[3] Bartlett, his daughter Priscilla[4] Bartlett, her daughter Susanna[4] Sampson (John[3], Stephen[2], Henry[1]), her son Peleg[5] Wadsworth (Peleg[4], John[3], JOHN[2], CHRISTOPHER[1]), and his daughter Zilpha[6] Wadsworth, who was the mother of *Henry Wadsworth Longfellow* (1807-1882).

By the marriage of SARAH[3] BREWSTER, about 1656,
the name of BREWSTER was merged in that of BARTLETT; in 1738
the name of BARTLETT was merged in that of SPRAGUE; in 1812
the name of SPRAGUE was merged in that of HOPKINS, in 1847
the name of HOPKINS was merged in that of **MUNSEY**.

AUTHORITIES

1. The "Brewster Book."
2. Brown's "Pilgrim Fathers of New England."
3. Dexter's "The England and Holland of the Pilgrims."
4. Arber's "Story of the Pilgrim Fathers."
5. Hunter's "Founders of New Plymouth."
6. Steele's "Life of Brewster—The Chief of the Pilgrims."
7. Goodwin's "Pilgrim Republic."
8. Dexter's "The Pilgrims in Their Three Homes."
9. Bradford's "History of Plymouth Plantation."
10. "Brewster Genealogy."

In the *New England Family History*, III, 411-421 is an extended bibliography of works pertaining to the Brewsters.

THE BROWN FAMILY

1. JOHN[1] BROWN, son of Richard Brown of Barton Regis, County Gloucester, England, married MARGARET, daughter of FRANCIS HAYWARD, of Bristol, England, and settled near Pemaquid Point, Maine, at the head of New Harbor, in what is now the town of Bristol, in the county of Lincoln, Maine. The *Magazine of American History* says he was a brother-in-law of John Pierce, and related to the Pierce family of Muscongus, who settled there, it is believed, in 1621; while BROWN was doubtless an old resident of the ancient Popham Fort of 1614. Others think he was sent as a planter to New England by Jennens or John Pierce under authority derived from the Plymouth Colony. At any rate, he was one of the first settlers at New Harbor. By a deed, dated July fifteenth, 1625, he bought of Samoset (or Somerset), the Indian sagamore who welcomed the Pilgrims at Plymouth, and Unnongoit, another sagamore, a tract of land embracing a large part of Lincoln County and including Muscongus Island. This immense tract extended back twenty-five miles from the sea and was eight miles wide on the rear line. The original deed is supposed to have been burned in the Boston Court House in 1748. The price paid for this princely tract was "50 Skins," which the Indians received "to their full satisfaction." This was the *first deed of conveyance on American soil*. The existence of this deed gave rise to numerous claims by BROWN's heirs.

These claims, with others, such as Hawthorne refers to in his *House of the Seven Gables,* were finally settled by a commission in 1813; and so ended "the last great controversy respecting landtitles in Maine."

JOHN[1] BROWN resided at New Harbor until the time of his death, which took place after the year 1660. The children of JOHN[1] and MARGARET (HAYWARD) BROWN were:

1. Elizabeth[2] Brown, who married Richard Pierce.
2. Margaret[2] Brown, who married Alexander ("Sander") Gould.
3. EMMA[2] BROWN, who married NICHOLAS[1] DENNING (1645-1725).
4. John[2] Brown, born 1635; living in 1721.

By the marriage of EMMA[2] BROWN

the name of BROWN   was merged in that of DENNING; in 1700

the name of DENNING   was merged in that of DAY;   in 1763

the name of DAY   was merged in that of SPRAGUE; in 1812

the name of SPRAGUE   was merged in that of HOPKINS in 1847

the name of HOPKINS was merged in that of MUNSEY.

AUTHORITIES

1. *New England Historical and Genealogical Register,* Vols. 13:365; 31:185.
2. "Lincoln County (Maine) Land Troubles," p. 17.
3. "Coll. of Maine Hist. Soc.", 1st Series, Vols. 1, 2, 4, 5, 7, 9.
4. *Magazine of American History,* 8:824.
5. Goodwin's "Pilgrim Republic," p. 118.

THE CARPENTER FAMILY

When ALICE[1] CARPENTER first came to America, she was the Widow Southworth. But as through her son, CONSTANT[1], she was a

progenitor of the Munseys in the tenth generation, it seems fitting that a sketch of the
Carpenters be given here.

The family to which Alice belonged has been
traced back in England to ₉John Carpenter,
a member of Parliament in 1323. The line de-
scends through ₈Richard, ₇John, ₆John, ₅William,
₄James, ₃John, ₂William. The last named had
three sons, ₁Alexander (father of ALICE¹), William, and Richard ₁Alexander and his brothers
were Dissenters, and on account of religious
persecution went to Leyden from England. The
name of ₁Alexander's wife is unknown; he had
five daughters and possibly a son William.
Four of the daughters married in Leyden. One
of these, Agnes, died there before 1617; the other
three sooner or later emigrated to America. The
father, ₁Alexander, did not go with his married
daughters, but—with the unmarried daughters,
and probably all other members of his family—
returned to England, apparently to his old home,
Wrington, about eight miles from Bristol.

Julia Ann Carpenter (1583–1665) was married
in Leyden, July twenty-third, 1612, to George
Morton, of York, England. She came with her
husband to America in the *Ann*, in 1623. She
married (2) Manasseh Kempton; died at Plymouth in 1665.

Agnes Carpenter (1585±-1616±) was married
on April thirtieth, 1613, to DR. SAMUEL
FULLER of London. She was his second wife,
his first being Elsie Glascock. Agnes died

apparently before 1617, for in that year DR. FULLER married (3) Bridget Lee. He came over in the *Mayflower* in 1620.

ALICE[1] CARPENTER (1590-1670) married at Leyden, May twenty-eighth, 1613, Edward Southworth (see SOUTHWORTH family), and by him became the mother of two sons, CONSTANT[1] (born 1614±) and Thomas (born 1616). Through the former of these she is said to be the ancestress of all the Southworths in this country. Before 1623 her husband Edward died, and she turned her thoughts toward the new world. Leaving her young sons with friends, she came with her sister and brother-in-law (Mr. and Mrs. Morton) to America. She landed in July, 1623, and on the fourteenth of the following August became the wife of GOV. BRADFORD.

Mary Carpenter (1595-1686/7) had returned with her father to Wrington, England, from Leyden, unmarried. After the death of her mother, GOVERNOR BRADFORD and his wife, Mary's sister, wrote her an affectionate letter in 1645, requesting her to come to Plymouth and make her home with them. This letter is still extant. She came and lived at Plymouth many years. The record of her death is as follows:

Mary Carpenter, a member of the church at Duxbury, died at Plymouth, March 19/20, 1687, being newly entered into the ninety-first year of her age. *She was a Godly old maid,—never married.*

Priscilla Carpenter (1598-1689), was the youngest of the five daughters. She was twice married. Her first husband, William Wright, died about 1633. Her second husband was John Cooper, of Duxbury. She survived all her family, living until December twenty-ninth, 1689.

"To this family of daughters of Alexander Carpenter, our New England people, and indeed we may say our whole country, owe an hitherto unacknowledged debt."

By the marriage of ALICE[1] CARPENTER, in 1613,

the name of CARPENTER became merged in that of SOUTHWORTH, in 1658*
the name of SOUTHWORTH became merged in that of FREEMAN II(a); in 1719(b)
the name of FREEMAN II became merged in that of HOPKINS; and in 1847
the name of HOPKINS became merged in that of **MUNSEY**.

AUTHORITIES

1. *Transcript* Clippings, 1911.
2. Goodwin's "Pilgrim Republic."
3. *Mayflower Descendant*, vol. 3.
4. "The Carpenter Family in America."

THE COBB FAMILY

There were four Cobb families in America in early colonial times, each distinct and apparently unrelated to the others:

1. The Virginia family
2. The Barnstable family
3. The Taunton family
4. The Boston and Hingham family

---

*In 1623 the name of ALICE (CARPENTER) SOUTHWORTH was changed to BRADFORD; the **MUNSEYS**, however, descend from her only as a SOUTHWORTH.

(a) SAMUEL[2] FREEMAN (SAMUEL[1], of Watertown); not descended from EDMUND[1] FREEMAN, of Sandwich.

(b) In 1685 the same line of Freemans merged with **MUNSEY** through Pepper (q. v.), Mereen (1754), and HOPKINS (1784).

1. THOMAS[1] COBB, of Boston and Hingham, was probably the grandson of Thomas Cobb, Esq., of Wilts, England, who died shortly before 1644. He had two sons, Richard, who married Honor —— before his father's death; and Michael, who in a will, drawn in 1644, and proved in 1646, mentions his late father Thomas and his married brother Richard.

The recurrence of the names Thomas and Richard makes it somewhat probable that THOMAS[1] and RICHARD[2] of Boston and Hingham were the respective grandsons of Thomas and Richard of Wilts. The known dates heighten the probability. THOMAS[1] COBB is said to have married, in England, a lady named Bannister; but as yet this is not proved. His son RICHARD[2] was baptized at Banbury, England, August eleventh, 1666. In 1685 both father and son came to Boston. On September fourth of that year Thomas Skinner becomes surety to the town for THOMAS[1] COBB, blacksmith, and his family; thus it is probable that his wife, as well as his son, came with him. About 1692 he removed to Hingham, where he died January fourth, 1707/8.

2. RICHARD[2] COBB, of Boston and Hingham, was born, as we have seen, in England, in or about 1666, came to Boston in 1685. In that city, on September sixteenth, 1691, "Richard Cobb and Esther Bates were married by Samuel Sewall, Esq., Assistant."[*] ESTHER[3] BATE(s) was a daugh-

---

[*] See footnote on page 63.

ter of Joseph² Bate (Clement¹) and Esther²
Hilliard (William¹) of Hingham (see Bate(s)
family). In 1702± Richard² Cobb and his wife
also removed to Hingham, where he died June
first, 1709. He is called a "master mariner."
He lived at the harbor, probably on or near what
is now called Green Street.

Children:

1. Thomas³ Cobb, born March twenty-eighth, 1693; married, 1717, Mercy⁴ Freeman of Eastham.
2. Richard³ Cobb, born 1695; married (1) Ruth Beal, (2)
   Esther ——.
3. John³ Cobb, born 1698±; married Sarah (Derby) Dyer.
4. Esther³ Cobb, born 1700±; married (1) John Tower, (2)
   Elisha Tower.
5. Dorothy³ Cobb, born 1702; married (1) Isaac Gross, (2)
   Thomas Tower.
6. Abiah³ Cobb, born 1709; married (1) Abigail Corthell,
   (2) Sarah (Barstow) Ladd.

3. Thomas³ Cobb (Richard², Thomas¹) of Hingham
and Truro was born in Hingham on March
twenty-eighth, 1693. He was published on November fourteenth, 1717, as intending to marry
Mercy⁴ Freeman (Lieutenant Edmund³,
Major John², Edmund¹) of Eastham (see Freeman I family). They were later married, but the
record has not been found. After the birth of their
first child at Hingham they removed to Truro.
In the old north cemetery at Truro their gravestones are still standing, inscribed as follows:

Thos. Cobb d. 9 Feb. 1768, aged 76 years.
Marcy, wife of Thos. Cobb d. 2 Dec., 1759, in her 67th
year.

Shebnah Rich says of him: "Thomas Cobb

must have been a staid and vigilant person, as he was appointed to *correct* the boys" [in church].

Children:

1. Mercy[4] Cobb, baptized 1718 at Hingham; married, 1744, Asa Sellew.
2. Thomas[4] Cobb, born 1720 at Truro; married, 1742, Ruth Collins.
3. Richard[4] Cobb, born 1721/2; married, 1747, Elizabeth Treat.
4. Thomasine[4] Cobb, born 1723/4.
5. Joseph[4] Cobb, born 1726; married, 1750/1, Rachel (Treat) Mulford, sister to Elizabeth Treat.
6. Freeman[4] Cobb, born 1728; died 1758.
7. Elisha[4] Cobb, born 1730; married, 1759, Dorcas Drake of Chatham; he lived at Wellfleet.
8. BETTY[4] COBB, born December twenty-second, 1732; married, August twenty-eighth, 1755, SIMEON[5] HOPKINS.
9. Sarah[4] Cobb, born August fifteenth, 1735.

4. BETTY[4] COBB (THOMAS[3], RICHARD[2], THOMAS[1]) was born in Truro December twenty-second, 1732; on August twenty-eighth, 1755, she married SIMEON[5] HOPKINS (CALEB[4-3], GILES[2], STEPHEN[1]) (see HOPKINS LINE).

By the marriage of BETTY[4] COBB, in 1755, the name of COBB was merged in that of HOPKINS, and in 1847 the name of HOPKINS was merged in that of MUNSEY.

AUTHORITIES

1. Boston *Transcript*, July thirty-first, 1905.
2. Ninth and Tenth "Reports of the Record Commissioners of Boston."
3. Lincoln's "Hingham."
4. Hobart's "Abington."
5. Truro Gravestones.
6. Waters's "Genealogical Gleanings."
7. Rich's "Truro."

THE COLLIER FAMILY

1. WILLIAM[1] COLLIER, of Duxbury, was—to quote
Savage—"a Merchant of London, who came
over in 1633, having for several years acted as
one of the Adventurers. He had so generous a
spirit as not to be content with making a profit
by the enterprise of the Pilgrims unless he shared
their hardships. Whether he brought a wife
from home or had any here is doubtful, but
four daughters came, of excellent character."
Other authorities say that his wife JANE accompanied him. He was made a freeman at once,
and rose to great prominence. He was elected
Assistant Councillor of the Governor in 1634,
and was re-elected to the same office every year
(except 1653) until 1666. During at least two
sessions he was Acting Governor. He was one
of the commissioners appointed by Plymouth
Colony in 1643, to form a confederation of the
New England Colonies. "He appears to have
been the wealthiest man in Duxbury, being rated
as highest on the tax list." "He was a distinguished early settler and a great benefactor to
the colony." He was one of the first purchasers
of Dartmouth in 1652. He died in 1670. His
four daughters, whom Savage mentions, were:

1. SARAH[2].   2. Rebecca[2].   3. Mary[2].   4. ELIZABETH[2].

2.1. SARAH[2] COLLIER (WILLIAM[1]) was born in England in 1615±. On May fifteenth, 1634, she
married (1), LOVE[2] BREWSTER (ELDER
WILLIAM[1]) whom she survived (see BREW-

STER family). She married (2), Richard Parke. She died April 26 (May 6), 1691.

2.2. ELIZABETH[2] COLLIER (WILLIAM[1]) was also born in England, in 1617±. On November second, 1637, she married CONSTANT[1] SOUTHWORTH (see SOUTHWORTH family).

I By the marriage of SARAH[2] COLLIER, in 1634,
the name of COLLIER   was merged in that of BREWSTER, in 1656±
the name of BREWSTER   was merged in that of BARTLETT, in 1738
the name of BARTLETT   was merged in that of SPRAGUE, in 1812
the name of SPRAGUE   was merged in that of HOPKINS; and in 1847
the name of HOPKINS   was merged in that of **MUNSEY**.

II. By the marriage of ELIZABETH[2] COLLIER, in 1637,
the name of COLLIER   was merged in that of SOUTHWORTH, in 1658
the name of SOUTHWORTH   was merged in that of FREEMAN II; in 1719
the name of FREEMAN II   was merged in that of HOPKINS, and in 1847
the name of HOPKINS   was merged in that of **MUNSEY**.

AUTHORITIES

1. *Mayflower Descendant*, Vol. IV.
2. The Boston *Transcript*, August 18, 1913; also Vol. 12.
3. Goodwin's "Pilgrim Republic."
4. "Plymouth Court Orders," Vol. I.
5. "Brewster Genealogy," Vol. I.
6. Savage's "Genealogical Dictionary."

THE DAMON FAMILY

1. JOHN[1] DAMON, the founder of the Scituate family, came with his sister Hannah to the Colony of Plymouth probably as early as 1628. Their uncle, William Gilson, was their guardian. He

is referred to as "a man of education and talents." He held many offices of responsibility in the colony, being Assistant for several years.

In 1633 Gilson and several others settled in Scituate and laid out the village there. They were called "Men of Kent," since they came from Kent County, England. The principal street of the village they named Kent Street. In 1636, Gilson erected a windmill (perhaps the first in America) for grinding corn, being allowed by a special Act of the Colonial Court not above one-twelfth part as toll.

Gilson died in 1639, leaving legacies to his wife, his pastor, and John[1] and Hannah Damon, his nephew and niece. The Widow Gilson died in 1649, and leaving no children, the nephew and niece were recognized by the Plymouth Court as lawful heirs, since their mother was William Gilson's sister. John[1] succeeded to his uncle's residence in Kent Street. In 1644, he had married Catherine[2] Merritt (Henry[1]) (see Merritt family), by whom he had six children:

1. Deborah[2]   2. John[2]   3. Zachary[2] (died young)
4. Mercy[2]   5. Daniel[2]   6. Zachary* 2d[2]

In 1659, he married (2), Martha Howland, by whom also he had six children:

1. Experience[2]   2. Silence[2]   3. Ebenezer[2]
4. Ichabod[2]   5. Margaret[2]   6. Hannah[2]

John[1] Damon died in 1677, and his widow, Martha, was made executrix. She later married Peter Bacon of Taunton.

* Sometimes spelled Zachery.

2. ZACHARY[2] DAMON (JOHN[1]) of Scituate was born in 1654. By the Colonial Records, it appears that John[2] and ZACHARY[2] DAMON were soldiers in King Philip's War in 1676, and received grants of land. ZACHARY was promoted to be a Lieutenant. In 1679, he married MARTHA[2] WOODWORTH of Scituate (see WOODWORTH family). He died in 1730, aged seventy-six. His children were:

1. Martha[3] 2. John[3] 3. Zachary[3]
4. Daniel[3] 5. Mercy[3] 6. Hannah[3] 7. MEHITABLE[3]

3. MEHITABLE[3] DAMON (LIEUTENANT ZACHARY[2], JOHN[1]), was born in Scituate *in 1696*. Another Mehitable[4], her niece, daughter of Zachary[3] Damon and Mehitable Chittenden, is said by some to have married JONATHAN[4] MERRITT (JOHN[3-2], HENRY[1]), in 1727. But Mehitable[4], daughter of Zachary[3], was not born until June eighteenth, 1716, and in 1727 was only eleven years old. It is true MEHITABLE[3] was at that time thirty-one, and perilously near old maidenhood, but we submit that the elder Mehitable is more likely to have been JONATHAN[4]'s bride than was the eleven-year old daughter of Mehitable (Chittenden) Damon. (See MERRITT family.)

By the marriage of MEHITABLE[3] DAMON, in 1727, the name of DAMON was merged in that of MERRITT; in 1786 the name of MERRITT was merged in that of SAWYER; and in 1812 the name of SAWYER was merged in that of MUNSEY.

AUTHORITIES

1. *Mayflower Descendant*, Vol. I, II.
2. "The Damon Memorial."
3. *N. E. Historical and Genealogical Register*, Vols. 18, 19.
4. *Genealogical Advertiser*, IV, 91, 92.
5. Bodge's "Soldiers in King Philip's War.
6. "Scituate Vital Records."
7. Deane's "Scituate."

THE DAY FAMILY

The Day family seems to have originated in Wales. The name is derived from *Dee*—dark. Very possibly the family took its name from a river in Wales (*cf.* "The Miller of the Dee"). In colonial days there were nine Day families in New England, all apparently distinct. Robert of Cambridge and Hartford, 1634–1636; Robert of Ipswich, 1635; Nathaniel of Ipswich, 1637; Stephen of Cambridge, 1639; Wentworth of Boston, 1630; Matthew of Cambridge, 1645; Ralph of Dedham, 1645; Anthony of Gloucester, 1645; Emmanuel of Manchester, (Mass.), 1685.

I. Anthony[1] Day, of Gloucester, sailed from London, England, July sixteenth, 1635, in the *Paul*. He probably landed in Virginia, or the Carolinas, and thence moved north by land. We find him in Gloucester in 1645. In 1650 he married. His wife's first name was Susanna. Her maiden name is in dispute; some give it as Matchett, others as Ring. Circumstances seem to indicate the former is correct. His death is usually given as April twenty-third, 1707; but as his administrator gave bond on May thirteenth, 1708, he probably died in the latter year. On June twentieth, 1695, he made oath that he was eighty; therefore he was born about 1615. He had the following children:

1. Thomas[2]	2. Timothy[2]	3. John[2]
4. Ezekiel[2] (died young)	5. Ezekiel 2d[2]	6. Nathaniel[2]
7. Elizabeth[2]	8. Samuel[2]	9. Joseph[2]

2. THOMAS² DAY (ANTHONY¹), of Gloucester, was born in 1651. He married (1), December thirtieth, 1673, MARY LANGTON; (2), November twenty-fifth, 1706, Hannah Clark. He died January twenty-ninth, 1726. The children of THOMAS² and MARY (LANGTON) DAY were:

1. THOMAS³   2. Mary³   3. Joseph³   4. John³

The first wife of THOMAS² DAY, perished, together with her daughter Mary³, in a thunder storm, July eighteenth, 1706; they were both struck by lightning in the entry of their home.

3. THOMAS³ DAY (THOMAS², ANTHONY¹), of Gloucester, was born May twenty-seventh, 1675. He married, March seventh, 1700, MARY, daughter of NICHOLAS DENNING.

The year 1716, was a year sadly memorable in the annals of Gloucester. In August of that year five vessels and twenty men—estimated at one-tenth the tonnage and one-fifteenth of all male citizens—were lost on a fishing voyage to the Isle of Sables. Among the number were THOMAS³ DAY and George Denning, aged thirty. It is probable that George was the brother-in-law of THOMAS³ DAY.

THOMAS³ and MARY (DENNING) DAY had the following children:

1. Hepzibah⁴   2. JOSIAH⁴   3. Stephen⁴
4. Mary⁴   5. Thomas⁴   6. Jacob⁴

4. JOSIAH⁴ DAY (THOMAS³, THOMAS², ANTHONY¹), of Gloucester (Massachusetts), and Georgetown (Maine), was born in Gloucester January thir-

tieth, 1703.   On November twenty-ninth, 1730, he married MARY THOMAS, of Matinicus, Maine. As this marriage is on record in Gloucester, apparently JOSIAH[4] DAY was living there at the time.   He finally removed to Georgetown, Maine, and died there in 1758.   Of the children of JOSIAH[4] and MARY (THOMAS) DAY, we find the following:

1. Mary[5] (baptized in Gloucester).   2. Mary 2d[5] (baptized in Gloucester) (died young.)
3. MIRIAM[5] (born in Georgetown).   And probably
4. Josiah[5] (married Wealthy Blethen).

5. MIRIAM[5] DAY (JOSIAH[4], THOMAS[3], THOMAS[2], ANTHONY[1]) was born in Georgetown (Maine), in 1739.   On July thirtieth, 1757, she married (1), James Blethen, and removed to Cape Elizabeth. He died not long after, and she married (2), March second, 1763, LIEUTENANT WILLIAM[5] SPRAGUE (JETHRO[4], WILLIAM[3], JOHN[2], FRANCIS[1]) of Georgetown (see SPRAGUE family).   She died October fifth, 1836.

By the marriage of MRS. MIRIAM[5] (DAY) BLETHEN, in 1763, the family of DAY was merged in that of SPRAGUE; in 1812 the name of SPRAGUE was merged in that of HOPKINS; in 1847 the name of HOPKINS was merged in that of MUNSEY.

AUTHORITIES

1. Stackpole's "Durham."
2. Winsor's "Duxbury."
3. "Memorial of Sprague Family."
4. "Lincoln Co. (Maine) Probate Records."
5. "Georgetown (Maine) Records."
6. *Bangor Historical Magazine.*
7. *Maine Historic Society Collection, 2d Series.*
8. Gloucester Town and Church Records.

9. *N. E. Historical and Genealogical Register, Vol. IV.*
10. Babson's "Gloucester" and "Notes and Additions."
11. "Essex County Quarterly Court Records."
12. "Day Family of Hartford."
13. "American Ancestry, Vol. XI."
14. Pringle's "Gloucester."
15. Holton's "List of Emigrants"
16. MS. of J. Alphonso Day, in Historic-Genealogical Library.

THE FARRAR FAMILY

1. JACOB[1] FARRAR, with an elder brother, John, was among the original signers of a "Covenant" to preserve the "purity of religion" in Lancaster, Massachusetts, and to keep out "profane and scandalous persons." Lancaster was incorporated May eighteenth, 1653. On the twenty-fourth of the following September, John and JACOB[1] signed the covenant aforesaid. They came hither from England, apparently from Lancashire. JACOB[1] was probably over thirty at the time. He had married about 1640, and left a wife (ANNE ——) and four children in England, until he should prepare a home in the new world. In 1658 he sent for his family. In a valuation of the town property, shortly after this, there is the following record: "Jacob Farrar added when his wife came £168 7s. od."

During King Philip's War, in 1675, two of his sons were killed. The town was captured by the Indians February tenth, 1675/6, and most of the property destroyed. JACOB[1], with his family, took refuge in Woburn. On the eleventh of March nineteen townsmen, including JACOB[1]

Farrar, John[1] Houghton, John[2] Houghton, John[1] Prescott, and Thomas[1] Sawyer, addressed a "Humble Petition of the distressed people of Lancaster" to the Government. This is now on record in the Secretary's office. Two years later, August fourteenth, 1677, Jacob[1] Farrar died.

The children of Jacob[1] and Anne Farrar were:

1. John[2] 2. Jacob[2] (killed August twenty-second, 1675).
3. Henry[2] (killed February, tenth, 1675/6).
4. Mary[2]   5. Joseph[2].

The first four were born in England, the last in Lancaster. The widow of Jacob[1] became, March second, 1680, the third wife of John Sears of Boston.

2. Mary[2] Farrar (Jacob[1]) was born in England in 1648±. On February twenty-second, 1671/2, she married John[2] Houghton (John[1]), of Lancaster (see Houghton family). Her husband and her mother Anne administered the estate of her father.

By the marriage of Mary[2] Farrar, in 1671/2,
the name of Farrar was merged in that of Houghton; in 1700 the name of Houghton was merged in that of Sawyer; in 1812 the name of Sawyer was merged in that of MUNSEY.

AUTHORITIES

1. "The Farrar Family."
2. "Report to the Brown Association," by Columbus Smith.
3. Nourse, "Military Annals of Lancaster."
4. Savage, "Genealogical Dictionary."
5. Marvin, "History of Lancaster."
6. *N. E. Historical and Genealogical Register*, October, 1852.

THE FLAGG FAMILY

The original spelling of the family name FLAGG was FLEGG. This is an old English surname, derived, according to tradition, from one *Rawl Flegg*, a Norse viking, who settled in Norfolk about 868. The spelling was changed about 1700 by common consent, as being more pleasing to the ear.

1. THOMAS FLAGG, of Watertown, came from County Norfolk to America in the year 1637, enrolled as a servant to Richard Carver, of Scratby. The story is current in the family that he loved a maid below his station; that they eloped separately, agreeing to meet in America; and that they took passage in two ships that sailed in company—one in the *John and Dorothy*, the other in the *Rose*. Soon after their arrival, they married. Whether their romance is true or not, THOMAS married a maid whose surname is unknown, but whose Christian name was MARY. As early as 1641 he had settled in Watertown, where he became a landowner, and a citizen of prominence. He was probably the ancestor of all the Flaggs in this country. He was selectman for five years. He lost his left eye in a gunshot accident previous to 1659. He died February sixth, 1697/8, aged eighty-three. His wife MARY was born in 1619, and died in 1703. Their children were:

1. LIEUTENANT GERSHOM[2]   2. John[2]
3. Bartholomew[2]   4. Thomas[2]   5. William[2]

6. Michael²   7. Eleazar²   8. Elizabeth²
9. Mary²   10. Rebecca²   11. Benjamin²
12. Allen²

2. LIEUTENANT GERSHOM² FLAGG (THOMAS¹), of
Watertown and Woburn, was born in Watertown, April sixteenth, 1641. He married, April
fifteenth, 1668, HANNAH² LEPPIN(G)WELL (MI-
CHAEL¹) (see LEFFINGWELL family). He was admitted freeman May twenty-seventh, 1674. He
removed to Woburn and engaged in the tanning
business there. He was commissioned First
Lieutenant of the Woburn Company in King
William's War. In 1690, since the Indians committed many depredations in New Hampshire,
two companies of scouts were raised to put an
end to their ravages. On July sixth, 1690, the
scouts overtook the enemy at Wheelwright's
Pond, a beautiful sheet of water in the town of
Lee, New Hampshire. A bloody engagement
ensued in which three white officers, twelve men
and many Indians were slain. The three officers were Captain Wiswall, LIEUTENANT GER-
SHOM² FLAGG, and Sergeant Walker.

The children of LIEUTENANT GERSHOM² and
HANNAH (LEPPIN(G)WELL) FLAGG were:

1. Gershom³   2. Eleazer³   3. John³
4. HANNAH³   5. Thomas³ (died young)
6. Ebenezer³   7. Abigail³   8. Mary³
9. Thomas 2d³   10. Benoni³

3. HANNAH³ FLAGG (LIEUT. GERSHOM², THOMAS¹)
was born in Woburn, March twelfth, 1675. She
married, January ninth, 1695/6, HENRY³ GREEN

(Lieutenant Henry[2], Thomas[1]) (see Green family.)

Lieutenant Gershom[2] Flagg's son, John[3] Flagg, was the father of
Ebenezer[4] Flagg, who was the father of
Dr. Henry Collins[5] Flagg, who was the father of
Henry Collins[6] Flagg. His daughter,
Rachel Moore[7] Flagg, married Abram E. Gwynne. Their daughter, Alice[8] Gwynne, married Cornelius Vanderbilt, a grandson of the old Commodore

By the marriage of Hannah[3] Flagg, in 1695/6,

the name of Flagg	was merged in that of Green;	in 1731
the name of Green	was merged in that of Lee;	in 1759
the name of Lee	was merged in that of Merritt;	in 1786
the name of Merritt	was merged in that of Sawyer;	in 1812
the name of Sawyer	was merged in that of **MUNSEY**.	

AUTHORITIES

1. McClintock's "New Hampshire."
2. Hurd's "Strafford Co., New Hampshire."
3. Flagg Family Records.
4. "Eleazer Flagg," by C. A. Flagg.
5. Year Book, Society of Colonial Wars, 1895.
6. Bond's "Watertown."
7. Pope's "Pioneers of Massachusetts."
8. North's "Augusta, Maine."
9. Concord, Massachusetts, "Births, Marriages, and Deaths."
10. *American Ancestry*, Vol. XI.

THE FREEMAN I FAMILY

1. Edmund[1] Freeman, of Sandwich, came from England in 1635, in the ship *Abigail*. His wife's maiden name is not known, but at Graveley, Herts, England, on October thirteenth, 1617, the marriage of Edmund Freeman to Elizabeth

Gurney is recorded. Since Mrs. Freeman's first
name was Elizabeth, this is possibly the record
of the marriage of Edmund[1].

We find Edmund[1] at Saugus (Lynn), in the
year of his arrival. Later he removed to Plymouth, where he was admitted freeman, January
second, 1637. A few months later he, with nine
others, obtained permission to found the first
English town on the Cape—the town of Sandwich. As his portion of the land in that town
was larger than that of any other man, it is
probable that he was the leader of the colony.

He was a man of great consequence. He bore
the unusual title of "Mr."* He was Deputy
for Plymouth Colony in 1641, Assistant to
Governor Prence (two of whose daughters
Mr. Freeman's sons married) from 1640-1646.
He was a member of the Council of War in 1642;
was presiding officer of a court of three "to hear
and determine controversies and causes" in
Sandwich and the adjoining towns; and later
was selected as Judge. Of him we find an interesting sketch in the "History of Barnstable,"
a part of which runs as follows:

"Edmund Freeman of Lynn, one of the first
settlers of Sandwich, was a prominent man of
good business habits, liberal in politics and
tolerant in his religious opinions. He was a
member of the Sandwich church—the most
bigoted and intolerant in the colony—yet he

---

* See page 27.

did not imbibe the persecuting spirit .   .   .
of his brethren. In his intercourse with his
neighbors .   .   . he was very kind and
affectionate. His wife died February fourteenth, 1676. .   . He was then eighty-six,
and had been married fifty-nine years." He
died in 1682, being then, it is believed, ninety-
two years of age.

All the descendants of EDMUND[1] FREEMAN'S
sons are eligible to membership in the Society
of *Mayflower* Descendants and the various
Colonial War Societies.

The children of EDMUND[1] and ELIZABETH
FREEMAN were:

1. Alice[2]   2. Edmund[2]   3. Elizabeth[2]
4. JOHN[2]   5. Mary[2]

2. MAJOR JOHN[2] FREEMAN (EDMUND[1]), of Sandwich and Eastham, was born in England, 1627±.
On February thirteenth, 1649/50, he married
MERCY[2] PRENCE (GOVERNOR THOMAS[1]) (see
PRINCE family). Just before or after this he
removed to Eastham, where he is mentioned in
the records as "among the earliest settlers, with
GOVERNOR PRENCE," his father-in-law. He was
prominent in public affairs, and "to this day has
been regarded as 'one of the fathers of Eastham' ". His record in the Indian wars is remarkable. He is said to have been an Ensign
in 1654; in 1671, July eighth, he was Lieutenant
and second in command in the expedition against
the Indians at Saconnet, when Major Josiah
Winslow, with one hundred and two men

marched against Awashonk, the Squaw Sachem;
he was Captain in the battle with the Indians at
Taunton in 1675; he was a member of the Council of War in 1675-6; and in 1685 was chosen
Major of the third Plymouth Colony Regiment,
composed of companies from Barnstable, Eastham, Sandwich, and Yarmouth.

His political services were equally noteworthy. He was Deputy eight years, from
1654; Selectman ten years, from 1663; Assistant several years, from 1666; and still later,
December seventh, 1692, he was appointed a
Judge of the Court of Common Pleas. He was
for the greater part of his life a Deacon of the
Church of Eastham.

He was a large land owner throughout his
career. Among the numerous recorded instru-
ments, to and from him, is a mortgage made in
1691, to him, of two islands for seventy-six
pounds, by the town of Eastham; that being
"the town's proportion of the expenses of getting
the new charter from England."

His wife died first, September twenty-eighth,
1711, aged eighty. On her curiously wrought
gravestone a heart is carved, within which is her
epitaph. MAJOR FREEMAN died October twenty-eighth, 1719. His gravestone says he was in
the ninety-eighth year of his age. That probably
is an error, as he appears to have been only
ninety-two.

The children of Major John[2] and Mercy[2] (Prence) Freeman were:

1. John[3] (died young)	2. John 2d[3]	3. Thomas[3]
4. Patience[3]	5. Hannah[3]	6. Edmund[3]
7. Mercy[3]	8. William[3]	9. Prince[3]
10. Bennet[3]	11. Nathaniel[3]	

3. Lieutenant Edmund[3] Freeman (Major John[2], Edmund[1]), of Eastham (Tonset), was born in June, 1657. He is believed to have married (1), Ruth Merrick; if so, his daughter Ruth (born 1680±), may have been by this marriage. But most of his children were by (2), Sarah[3] Mayo (Captain Samuel[2], Reverend John[1]) (see Mayo family). He was a man of prominence in town affairs, and for many years one of the selectmen. He died December tenth, 1717. His wife survived him until 1745. He had three sons and nine daughters:

1. Ruth[4]	2. Sarah[4]	3. Mary[4]
4. Isaac[4]	5. Ebenezer[4]	6. Edmund[4]
7. Experience[4]	8. Mercy[4]	9. Thankful[4]
10. Elizabeth[4]	11. Hannah[4]	12. Rachel[4]

4. Mercy[4] Freeman I, (Lieutenant Edmund[3], Major John[2], Edmund[1]) was born in Eastham in 1696±; on October fourteenth, 1717, she married Thomas[3] Cobb (Richard[2], Thomas[1]), of the same town (see Cobb family).

By the marriage of Mercy[4] Freeman I, in 1717,
the name of Freeman I was merged in that of Cobb; in 1755
the name of Cobb   was merged in that of HOPKINS;
and in 1847
the name of HOPKINS was merged in that of MUNSEY.

AUTHORITIES

1. "New England Family History," Vol. 2.
2. *Boston Transcript*, May fifth, 1913; August fifteenth, 1913.
3. Savage, "Genealogical Dictionary."
4. *N. E. Historical and Genealogical Register*, Vols. 4, 6, 9, 20.
5. *Mayflower Descendant*, Vols. 3, 5, 6.
6. "Society of the Colonial Wars—Illinois," 1900; Yearbook, 1894.
7. "Plymouth Colony Records," 1:140; 3:74-174; 4:147.
8. "Freeman Genealogy."
9. "Mayo Genealogy" (in MS. in Hist.-Gen. Soc. Library).

THE FREEMAN II FAMILY

1. SAMUEL[1] FREEMAN, of Watertown, came from England to America at the same time with Gov. Winthrop, in 1630, though perhaps not in the same vessel. He was in Watertown that same year, a landowner and a householder. On February eleventh, 1630/1, his house was burned. His wife's name was APPHIA. In 1639 MR. FREEMAN returned to England on business, and while there was taken sick and died. His widow later married GOVERNOR PRENCE. The children of SAMUEL[1] and APPHIA FREEMAN were:

    1. Henry[2]   2. Apphia[2]   3. SAMUEL[2]

2. DEACON SAMUEL[2] FREEMAN (SAMUEL[1]) of Eastham was born in Watertown, May eleventh, 1638, but removed to Eastham. He married, May twelfth, 1658, when he was barely twenty years old, MERCY[2] SOUTHWORTH (CONSTANT[1]) (see SOUTHWORTH family). MR. FREEMAN became a deacon of the Eastham church in 1676. He was

chosen Representative in 1697. "A man of pecuniary resources and of financial ability, he was of service to the town in times of peculiar straits." He died November twenty-fifth, 1712, aged seventy-five. The children of DEACON SAMUEL² and MERCY² (SOUTHWORTH) FREEMAN were:

1. Apphia³ (died young)   2. Samuel³   3. APPHIA (2D)³
4. CONSTANT³   5. Elizabeth³   6. Edward³
7. Mary³   8. Alice³   9. Mercy³

3.1. APPHIA (2D)³ FREEMAN (DEACON SAMUEL², SAMUEL¹) was born in 1666; in 1685 she married ISAAC² PEPPER (ROBERT¹).

> By the marriage of APPHIA (2ᵈ)³ FREEMAN II, in 1685,
>   the name of FREEMAN II was merged in that of PEPPER*; in 1754
>   the name of PEPPER   was merged in that of MEREEN;   in 1784
>   the name of MEREEN   was merged in that of HOPKINS, in 1847
>   the name of HOPKINS was merged in that of MUNSEY.

3.2. CAPTAIN CONSTANT³ FREEMAN (DEACON SAMUEL², SAMUEL¹), of Truro was born in Eastham, March thirty-first, 1669. He married, October eleventh, 1694, JANE⁴ TREAT (REVEREND SAMUEL³, GOVERNOR ROBERT², RICHARD¹) of Eastham (see TREAT family). In 1705 he moved to Truro (Pamet), his grandfather Southworth having given him one-sixteenth of the township. He was the first treasurer of Truro; a Representative to the General Court; selectman for seven years; and a captain of militia. He was a very prominent citizen. He

---

* The name of FREEMAN II reaches the *Munseys* by a shorter road under 4 below. Cf. pages 84 and 89.

was one of the founders of the church in **Truro** in 1711, and a deacon from 1718 to 1727, when he was made a ruling elder. He paid five pounds, ten shillings (higher than any other person), for his pew in the new meeting house. He died at Truro, June eighth, 1795, aged seventy-six.

The children of CAPTAIN CONSTANT[3] and JANE[4] (TREAT) FREEMAN were:

1. Robert[4]	2. Jane[4] (died young)	
3. Jane 2d[4]	4. Constant[4]	5. MERCY[4]
6. Hannah[4]	7. Eunice[4]	8. Elizabeth[4]
9. Jonathan[4]	10. Apphia[4]	11. Joshua[4]

4. MERCY[4] FREEMAN II (CAPTAIN CONSTANT[3], DEACON SAMUEL[2], SAMUEL[1]) was born in Eastham, August thirty-first, 1702. She married (1), October eighth, 1719, CALEB[4] HOPKINS (CALEB[3], GILES[2], STEPHEN[1]) (see HOPKINS LINE). After his death, in 1741, she married (2), June twenty-eighth, 1749, Benjamin Higgins; and (3), December fifth, 1771, Ebenezer Dyer. She died in December, 1786, aged eighty-four.

By the marriage of MERCY[4] FREEMAN II, in 1719,
  the name of FREEMAN II was merged in that of HOPKINS;
  and in 1847
  the name of HOPKINS was merged in that of **MUNSEY.**

AUTHORITIES

1. Savage, "Genealogical Dictionary."
2. Pope, "Pioneers of Massachusetts."
3. *Mayflower Descendant,* Vol. 6.
4. *N. E. Historical and Genealogical Register,* Vol. 6.
5. "Freeman Genealogy."
6. *New England Family History.*
7. "Treat Family."

THE GREEN FAMILY

1. THOMAS[1] GREEN, of Malden,was born in England, in 1606±. The first record in this country in which his name appears is in 1653, when his youngest daughter, Dorcas, was born. Yet there are indications that he came to this country several years earlier (probably in 1635±), and lived in Ipswich. He had a farm of sixty-three acres in North Malden, now Melrose. Part of this farm is still in the possession of his descendants. He was a selectman of Malden in 1658, and was several times on the grand jury of Middlesex County. There were two other Thomas Greens in Malden at that time. To distinguish them, the subject of this sketch was called *Thomas Green, Senior;* his son, *Thomas Green, Junior;* while the third was denominated plain *Thomas Green.*

THOMAS[1] GREEN married (1), Elizabeth ———, who died, August twenty-second, 1658; (2), Mrs. Frances (———) [Wheeler-Cook]. He died December nineteenth, 1667, leaving an estate valued at two hundred eighty-six pounds. His children, all by his first wife, and four or five of them probably born in England, were:

1. Elizabeth[2]	2. Thomas[2]	3. John[2]
4. Mary[2]	5. William[2]	6. HENRY[2]
7. Samuel[2]	8. Hannah[2]	9. Martha[2]
10. Dorcas[2]		

2. LIEUTENANT HENRY[2] GREEN (THOMAS[1]), of Malden, was born in Ipswich, in 1638. He married,

January eleventh, 1671/2, ESTHER[2] HASEY ("HASSE"), who was born 1649/50. She was daughter of LIEUTENANT WILLIAM[1] HASEY, who died in 1689. LIEUTENANT GREEN was a selectman thirteen years and Representative four times. He died in Malden, September nineteenth, 1717, aged seventy-eight. His wife survived him thirty years, dying in Stoneham, February twenty-sixth, 1747/8, at the age of ninety-eight. Their children were:

1. HENRY[3]   2. Esther[3]   3. Joseph[3]
4. Daniel[3]   5. Dorcas[3]   6. Lydia[3]
7. Jacob[3]

3. HENRY[3] GREEN (LIEUTENANT HENRY[2], THOMAS[1]), of Stoneham, Massachusetts, and Killingly, Connecticut, was born in Malden, January twenty-fourth, 1672/3. He married HANNAH[3] FLAGG (LIEUTENANT GERSHOM[2], THOMAS[1]), of Woburn on January ninth, 1695/6 (see FLAGG family). She was born March twelfth, 1675.

MR. GREEN lived for a time in that part of Charlestown which is now called Stoneham. On January thirtieth, 1718/9, he sold his brother Daniel[3] about ninety acres of land in Charlestown (Stoneham) and Malden for seven hundred sixty pounds. Soon after this he removed to Killingly (now Thompson), Windham County, in northeastern Connecticut, whither many Massachusetts people emigrated in the first part of the eighteenth century. HENRY[3] GREEN with his eight sons became the first resident proprietors of the town in the vicinity of

"Quadic."   He was No. 17 of the twenty-seven constituent members of the Thompson Congregational church (organized January twenty-eighth, 1730), and heads the list of the seventeen pewholders.   He was living in 1740, and probably died in Killingly.   The children of HENRY[3] and HANNAH[3] (FLAGG) GREEN were:

1 and 2. Henry[4] and Ebenezer[4] (twins)   3. Hannah[4]
4. Seth[4]   5. Eleazer[4]   6. Nathan[4]
7. Timothy[4]   8. ESTHER[4]   9. Phinehas[4]
10. Amos[4]   11. Abigail[4]

4. ESTHER[4] GREEN (HENRY[3], LIEUTENANT HENRY[2], THOMAS[1]) of Killingly was born in Charlestown, May seventeenth, 1708.   When she was about ten years of age she removed with her parents and her ten brothers and sisters to Killingly (Thompson), Connecticut.   There she married August fifteenth, 1731, ISAAC[2] LEE, son of SAMUEL[1] LEE, formerly of Watertown.

By the marriage of ESTHER[4] GREEN, in 1731,
    the name of GREEN   was merged in that of LEE;   in 1759
    the name of LEE   was merged in that of MERRITT;   in 1786
    the name of MERRITT was merged in that of SAWYER;   in 1812
    the name of SAWYER   was merged in that of MUNSEY.

AUTHORITIES

1. S. S. Greene's "Thomas Green, of Malden."
2. *N. E. Historical and Genealogical Register*, Vols. 37, 42.
3. "Year Books" of Society of Colonial Wars, 1875, 1896.
4. Malden "Vital Records."
5. "Historical Address" (July fourth, 1876), by E. H. Goss in Melrose.
6. "History of Tolland and Windham Counties, Connecticut."
7. E. H. Goss's "History of Melrose."
8. "History of Windham County, Connecticut."
9. Thompson (Connecticut) Congregational "Church Manual."

THE HIGGINS FAMILY

1. RICHARD[1] HIGGINS of Eastham, tailor, was taxed in Plymouth in 1632. On October seventh, 1633, he bought a house of Thomas Little for twenty-one bushels of corn. He was made a freeman in 1634. On December eleventh, 1634, he married (1) LYDIA[2], daughter of EDMUND[1] CHANDLER. On August eighteenth, 1645, he sold out his possessions in Plymouth to John Churchwell and went to Eastham. In 1647-51 he was a Representative to the General Court. The date of his first wife's death is unknown; but in October, 1651, he married (2) Mary Yates. His children were:

By LYDIA[2] CHANDLER:

1. Jonathan[1]   2. BENJAMIN[2]

By Mary Yates:

1. Mary[2]   2. Eliakim[2]   3. Jadiah[2]
4 Zera (Zeruiah)[2]   5. Thomas[2]   6. Lydia[2]

2. BENJAMIN[2] HIGGINS (RICHARD[1]), of Eastham, was born in Plymouth in June, 1640. He moved in early childhood to Eastham, and there, on December twenty-fourth, 1661, married LYDIA[2] BANGS (EDWARD[1]) (see BANGS family). He died March fourteenth, 1691, his wife surviving him. In the settlement of his estate, as agreed to, on June twenty-fourth, 1691, seven of his nine children (all but Nos. 3 and 7), are named. The entire list follows:

1. Ichabod[3]   2. Richard[3]   3. John[3]
4. Joshua[3]   5. Lydia[3]   6. ISAAC[3]
7. Rebecca[3]   8. Samuel[3]   9. Benjamin[3]

It is possible that No. 7 should be, "Benjamin, born 1675; died young."

3. ISAAC[3] HIGGINS (BENJAMIN[2], RICHARD[1]) of Eastham was born on August thirty-first, 1672. He married LYDIA[2] COLLINS (JOSEPH[1]) at a date unknown. The will of JOSEPH[1] COLLINS mentions his daughter LYDIA HIGGINS and a son-in-law ISAAC HIGGINS.

The children of ISAAC[3] and LYDIA[2] (COLLINS) HIGGINS were:

1. Mary[4]	2. Sarah[4]	3. Benjamin[4]
4. Elkanah[4]	5. REBECCA[4]	6. Isaac[4]
7. Hannah[4]	8. Lydia[4]	

4. REBECCA[4] HIGGINS (ISAAC[3], BENJAMIN[2], RICHARD[1]) of Eastham was born October tenth, 1705. The date of her marriage, like that of her mother, is unknown, but the *fact* is proved by her father's will. Her husband was JOSEPH[3] PEPPER (ISAAC[2], ROBERT[1]).

By the marriage of REBECCA[4] HIGGINS
the name of HIGGINS was merged in that of PEPPER; in 1754
the name of PEPPER was merged in that of MEREEN; in 1784
the name of MEREEN was merged in that of HOPKINS, in 1847
the name of HOPKINS was merged in that of MUNSEY.

AUTHORITIES

1. *Transcript* clippings—1911.
2. *N. E. Historical and Genealogical Register*, Vol. 6.
3. Savage, "Genealogical Dictionary."
4. *Mayflower Descendant*, Vol. 5.
5. "Barnstable Probate Record," 4:171-2, 192.
6. Will of Isaac Higgins, of Eastham (February twelfth, 1760).

THE HOUGHTON FAMILY

In 1635 the *Abigail*, 300 tons, sailed from London with many passengers for New England. Among these was ₁JOHN HOUGHTON. He was christened May nineteenth, 1593, in St. Mary's Church at Eaton Bray, England, where his father ₂JOHN HOUGHTON was buried, April twenty-eighth, 1618. The following is from the passenger list:

20th June, 1635, passenger from London to New England in ship "Abigail," Hackwell Master, John Houghton, 40 years old; certificate of his conformity from justices of the peace and minister [of] Eaton Bray, in County Bedford, England.

This ₁JOHN HOUGHTON is not the pioneer, for he later returned to England; but his son—

1. JOHN¹ HOUGHTON, of Lancaster, Massachusetts, was born in England in 1624±. He came to Dedham, Massachusetts, from England between 1648 and 1652. Some say he was married before he came; others that he married his wife, BEATRIX ——, in Dedham. The oldest date to be found in Lancaster is that over his grave. His tombstone in the Old Granary Burying Ground says he died on the old Common, April twenty-ninth, 1684, aged sixty years. He had a very large landed estate. After the Indian massacre of 1676, he removed to Woburn, where he remained some years; but later he returned

to Lancaster. The children of JOHN[1] and
BEATRIX HOUGHTON were:

1. JOHN[2]   2. Robert[2]   3. Jonas[2]
4. Mary[2]   5. Beatrix[2]   6. Benjamin[2]
7. Sarah[2]

2. JOHN[2] HOUGHTON (JOHN[1]) of Lancaster was either
   born in England and came with his parents to
   America about 1650; or he was born in Dedham,
   Mass., perhaps a little earlier. He became the
   most prominent man of his day in Lancaster.
   He represented the town in the General Court
   from 1693 to 1724 inclusive. He was commonly
   called Justice Houghton, and for a long time
   was the only magistrate in town. He was celebrated as a man of weight and influence, and was
   a skillful conveyancer. Three pear trees which
   he planted still stand (1896), before the site of
   his house. During the last twelve years of his
   life he was blind.

   He married (1), January twenty-second,
   1671/2, MARY[2] FARRAR (JACOB[1]) (see FARRAR
   family). She was born in 1648, in Lancashire,
   England, and died at Lancaster, Massachusetts,
   in 1724. MR. HOUGHTON married (2), at the
   age of seventy-five, Hannah Wilder, aged seven-
   ty-two.

   He died February third, 1737, in the eighty-
   seventh year of his age. The epitaphs of JOHN[2]
   HOUGHTON and his first wife MARY[2] FARRAR are
   still legible upon their tombstones, as follows:

Here lies buried
yᵉ body of
John Houghton
esquir, as you are so ware we
as we are so
you will be
who died February yᵉ 3ᵈ anno dominy
1736-7 and
in yᵉ 87ᵗʰ year
of his age.

Here lies
buried yᵉ body
of *Mrs. Mary
Houghton* yᵉ
wife of *John
Houghton* esquir
who died April
yᵉ 7ᵗʰ ano dm 1724
and in the 76ᵗʰ year
of her age

The children of JOHN[2] and MARY[2] (FARRAR) HOUGHTON were:

1. Lieut. John[3]   2. Jacob[3]   3. Henry[3]
4 and 5. Joseph[3] and Benjamin[3] (twins)
6. MARY[3] ("born 6-18-1668"; but as the *twins* were born 1678 and *Mercy* in 1682, "1668" is evidently a typographical error for 1680).
7. Mercy[3]   8. Anna[3]   9. Jonathan[3]
10. Hepzibah[3]   11. Rebecca[3]   12. Beatrix[3]
13. William[3]

3. MARY[3] HOUGHTON (JOHN[2], JOHN[1]), was born in Lancaster in 1680. In 1700 she married WILLIAM[3] SAWYER (THOMAS[2], THOMAS[1]) of the same town (see SAWYER family). She died in 1754.

By the marriage of MARY[3] HOUGHTON, in 1700,
    the name of HOUGHTON was merged in that of SAWYER; in 1812
    the name of SAWYER   was merged in that of MUNSEY.

AUTHORITIES

1. "The Houghton Genealogy."
2. "History and Genealogy of the Houghton Family." (Halifax, 1896).
3. "Sawyer Family in America."

THE HYLAND FAMILY

1. THOMAS[1] HYLAND (Heilland, Hiland), of Scituate, was baptized at Waldron, England, April twenty-third, 1604. He died in New England between February fourteenth, 1682/3 and May third, 1683. He married DEBORAH —— and lived in Tenterden, England, from 1629 to 1636. Then he emigrated to New England, where he was a proprietor in Scituate in 1637. He took the oath of allegiance on February first, 1638/9, and was later a juryman and town officer. He left to his son, THOMAS[2], lands in Waldron and a house in Tenterden. There is a "Hyland's Farm" in Waldron to-day, and a Hyland keeps a dry-goods shop in Tenterden. The children of THOMAS[1] and DEBORAH HYLAND were:

1. THOMAS[2]	2. Mary[2]	3. Elizabeth[2]
4. Sarah[2]	5. Annah[2]	6. Samuel[2]
7. Deborah[2]	8. Ruth[2]	

2. THOMAS[2] HYLAND (THOMAS[1]), of Scituate was born in Tenterden, England, where he was baptized on November fifteenth, 1629. He came

with his parents to New England after 1636. On January first, 1660/1, he married ELIZABETH² STOCKBRIDGE (JOHN¹). He died after 1683.

The children of THOMAS² and ELIZABETH² (STOCKBRIDGE) HYLAND were:

1. Thomas³   2. ELIZABETH³   3. Mary³
4. John³   5. Ruth³

3. ELIZABETH³ HYLAND (THOMAS², THOMAS¹) was born in Scituate, August fifteenth, 1665, but was not baptized until the twenty-fourth of September. In 1686 she married JOHN³ MERRITT (JOHN², HENRY¹) of the same town (see MERRITT family).

By the marriage of ELIZABETH³ HYLAND, in 1686,
    the name of HYLAND   was merged in that of MERRITT, in 1786
    the name of MERRITT   was merged in that of SAWYER; in 1812
    the name of SAWYER   was merged in that of MUNSEY.

AUTHORITIES

1. *Genealogical Advertiser.*
2. *N. E. Historical and Genealogical Register*, Vols. 19 and 66.
3. *Mayflower Descendant*, Vol. 2.
4. Scituate "Vital Records."

THE JACKSON FAMILY

1. DR. GEORGE¹ JACKSON appears first in Marblehead, Massachusetts. His origin is unknown. Farmer says of him: "GEORGE JACKSON, a surgeon of Marblehead, accompanied the Phips expedition to Canada, 1690, in that capacity [of surgeon]; purchased a farm in Scituate,

August, 1702." Savage adds that he had a wife
MARY.

The latter statement is true, for the Marblehead "Vital Records" declare: GEORGE JACKSON
married MARY NICK, December eighth, 1690.
He may have bought a farm, also, in Scituate,
but there is no evidence that he ever lived there.

The wife of DR. GEORGE[1] JACKSON was a
double widow. Her father was SAMUEL ABORN
of Salem (see ABORN family), whose will, dated
July twentieth, 1699, was not admitted to probate; but the Essex Probate records refer to his
daughter, "Mary, the wife of DR. GEORGE
JACKSON, of Marblehead."

MARY (ABORN) [Starr-Nick] JACKSON's prior
husband, William Nick, made his will October
fifteenth, 1683. It was probated on the thirtieth of the next month. He mentions the
children of his "wife that is now, viz., her
children Mary Starr, Sarah Starr, Rebecca
Starr, and Hannah Starr." The inference is
plain: Mary Aborn married (1), a Mr. Starr,
(2), William Nick, and (3), DR. GEORGE[1]
JACKSON. By all husbands she had children;
for William Nick's will, after disposing of the
first galaxy, goes on to mention "my child
William Nick and the child she now goeth
withal." He made his wife executrix, and mentioned his "father-in-law, SAMUEL ABORN."
Thirteen years after William Nick's death, in
1696, DR. GEORGE[1] JACKSON and his wife MARY

made their accounting of her former husband's estate.

DR. JACKSON was among the foremost citizens of his town. In 1707, Col. Francis Nicholson and thirty-three other gentlemen (twenty-nine being captains of vessels), subscribed a building fund of one hundred seventy-five pounds toward the erection of an Episcopal Church in Marblehead. There was then but one church of that faith in Massachusetts—King's Chapel, Boston. In 1711 another Episcopal church was built in Newbury, but the edifice in Marblehead had not yet been begun. Finally, on March thirty-first, 1714, GEORGE[1] JACKSON, SR., headed a supplementary subscription list with twenty pounds, with a promise to erect a building as soon as possible. Thirty-nine other gentlemen signed after him, the total amount pledged being three-hundred seventy-three pounds and ten shillings. On July twentieth, 1714, GEORGE[1] JACKSON and three others were elected a standing committee "on that affair in building a Handsome Church." They wasted no time; for on September second, 1714, "the committee erected and raised a church" which was later named St. Michael's. It still stands—one of the oldest church edifices in America and the very oldest Episcopal church building in the United States, except perhaps, "Old Trinity," of Newport, R. I. The King's Chapel and Newbury Church, built before this, were burned and rebuilt at a later date. The mural monument of the founder, Col. Nicholson, contains also the name of GEORGE[1] JACKSON and his three associates.

DR. JACKSON died in 1724. His will of August twenty-fourth, 1722, with a codicil of July twenty-third, 1723, was probated April twentieth, 1724. His wife, MARY, had died March twenty-third, 1721/2. The will left all his property to his three sons:

1. Bartholomew[2]   2. GEORGE[2]   3. John[2]

2. DR. GEORGE[2] JACKSON (DR. GEORGE[1]), of Kittery and Salem, was born in 1692. The "New England Family History" says: "Dr. J. L. M. Willis, in *Old Eliot*, puts DR. GEORGE JACKSON as the fourth physician in Kittery in 1724, and adds (speaking of DR. JACKSON): 'He appears in history as one who with Mr. Cutt and twenty men of Kittery pursued a party of Indians into Penobscot Bay. The Doctor and Mr. Cutt were dangerously wounded, but both recovered.'"

DR. JACKSON later removed to Salem. In 1730 the neighboring town of Marblehead was stricken with a plague of smallpox. The people were terror-stricken. No egress was allowed to those living in the town, and they were shunned like lepers. But DR. JACKSON was not derelict in his duty as a minister of mercy, for the simple entry found in Felt's "Annals of Salem" shows that he attacked the dread disease with the same courage with which he pursued the hostile Indians:

"1730, October 16. Doct. Geo. Jackson, of

Salem, hath visited the people of Marblehead, sick with the small pox."

On March twenty-seventh, 1711, Dr. Jackson married Joanna² Pepperrell, sister of the baronet, Sir William Pepperrell (see Pepperrell family). The children of Dr. George² and Joanna² (Pepperrell) Jackson were:

1. Margery³   2. Mary³   3. Elizabeth³
4. Joanna³   5. Dorothy³   6. Sarah³

By 1760 *all* the sons of Dr. George¹ Jackson were dead. Dr. George² died in 1735. On September twenty-fourth, 1762, Joanna³ (Jackson) Frost speaks of "My honored father, George² Jackson, late of Salem, deceased .   .   . [and] his father George¹ Jackson, late of Marblehead, physician."

3. Dorothy³ Jackson (Dr. George², Dr. George¹) of Salem in 1736, was married to Derry³ Pitman (Nathaniel², William¹) of Durham, N. H., (see Pitman family).

By the marriage of Dorothy³ Jackson, in 1736, the name of Jackson was merged in that of Pitman; in 1772* the name of Pitman was merged in that of MUNSEY.

AUTHORITIES

1. "New England Family History."
2. Willis's *Old Eliot.*
3. Essex "Probate Records."
4. Savage, "Genealogical Dictionary."
5. Farmer, "First Settlers of New England."

---

* About 1748 Pitman merged in Munsey by another line (*Abigail⁴* Pitman, *Zachariah³, Joseph², William¹*); page 147.

6. Pamphlet of "Exercises Commemorating the Restoration of St. Michael's Church, Marblehead, April 18, 1888."
7. "158th Anniversary of St. Michael's."
8. "Bi-Centennial of 1st Congregational Church in Marblehead."
9. Marblehead "Vital Records."
10. Felt, "Annals of Salem."
11. "Essex County Deeds," 120:234.
12. "Maine Wills," p. 342.
13. *Essex Antiquarian*, Vol. II.

THE LEFFINGWELL FAMILY

That the Leffingwells came from England there is no doubt, though for many years none of the name have been found there. Over four hundred years ago—in 1495—a Lawrence Leffingwell lived in England. Since that time the form of the name has often been changed. It became Levingwell, Leffyngwell, Lippingwell, Leppinwell, Leapphingwell, Lephingwell and Leapingwell. The last form was for a long time explained as denoting a *boiling spring*, the inference being that the original ancestor possessed one. But that theory has been discarded, and American Leffingwells have returned to the spelling which fifteenth century Lawrence employed.

English records show that on February nineteenth, 1603—the year when Queen Bess died—Michael, son of Thomas Leppin(g)well, was baptized. Very possibly this may have been the MICHAEL LEPPIN(G)WELL who was living in Boston in 1636, but shortly after removed to the town of Woburn. His name appears on the

Woburn tax list in 1645. He had ten children, only two of whom were sons. In fact, the male line from MICHAEL became extinct over a century ago, the name being merged in that of many other New England families. The Rev. E. B. Huntington, who began the collection of memoranda regarding the Leffingwells of America, believed MICHAEL was an older brother of the famous Thomas Leffingwell of Connecticut, who was the personal friend of Uncas, "The Last of the Mohicans."

ISABEL, wife of Michael, died November seventeenth, 1671; Michael died March twenty-second, 1687. They had the following children:

1. Hannah²	2. HANNAH²	3. Sarah²
4. Thomas²	5. Ruth²	6. Michael²
7. Rachel²	8. Abigail²	9. Hesther²
10. Tabitha²		

2. HANNAH² LEPPIN(G)WELL (MICHAEL¹) of Woburn married LIEUTENANT GERSHOM² FLAGG (THOMAS¹) April fifteenth, 1668 (see FLAGG family).

By the marriage of HANNAH² LEPPINGWELL, in 1668,
the name of LEPPINGWELL was merged in that of FLAGG; in 1696
the name of FLAGG   was merged in that of GREEN; in 1731
the name of GREEN   was merged in that of LEE; in 1759
the name of LEE   was merged in that of MERRITT; in 1786
the name of MERRITT was merged in that of SAWYER; in 1812
the name of SAWYER   was merged in that of MUNSEY.

AUTHORITIES

1. "The Leffingwell Record."
2. Woburn "Vital Records."
3. Savage, "Genealogical Dictionary."

THE McINTYRE FAMILY

(McIntire, Mackintire, Macantier, Mackentier, Mackintier, mCintire, etc.)

In the year 1729 Col. David Dunbar contrived to be appointed Governor of the Province of Sagadahoc, Maine. He settled at Pemaquid and invited his countrymen (Scotchmen from the north of Ireland) to settle in his province, offering them liberal inducements. He laid out three townships—now Boothbay, Bristol, and Nobleboro—and peopled them in two or three years with more than 150 families, most of them Scotch-Irish. With reference to this immigration William Willis says:

"Throughout three towns, and scattered far beyond, over the whole State, are the descendants of these colonists; and we trace in the respectable names of McCobb, Campbell, Montgomery, McClintock, Huston, McLean, McKeen, McFarland, Coldwell, Dick, Forbush, Brown and McINTYRE the offspring of men who once trod in pride and power the land 'of brown heath and shaggy wood,' who wandered on the beautiful banks of Ayr, or reposed in the shade of Ettrick, or mustered for the fray at the pibroch's spirit-stirring sound and the shrill slogan of the McGregor."

But Massachusetts then had jurisdiction over Maine, and she looked upon Colonel Dunbar as a sort of usurper. She accordingly contrived to have him recalled, and to have the charge of

affairs in the Pemaquid region entrusted to
Samuel Waldo, who had some personal interest
there, as a patentee of the portion between the
St. George and Penobscot Rivers. On this
portion Mr. Waldo determined to settle other
Scotch-Irish families, that they might readily
affiliate with their neighbors in and around
Pemaquid. Some of these families were new-
comers; others had been in America since 1719.
"It is said that seven of them, viz.: Alexander
McLean, WILLIAM[1] McINTYRE, James Howard,
Robert Spear and three others not recollected,
had previously been deputed, by their associates
in Boston and vicinity, to select a suitable place
for settlement; and that, after visiting Pemaquid, the Kennebec and other places, they were
so struck with the advantages of this river [St.
George's] as at once to give it the preference.
But whether this was previous to 1729 .   .   .
we are unable to state. Certain it is, that
twenty-seven persons [on their own behalf and
in behalf of seventeen others either at the time
absent or under age—among them WILLIAM[1]
McINTYRE] now entered into an agreement with
Mr. Waldo, dated St. George's Fort, April
eighteenth, 1735, by which they engaged to
settle themselves and families on St. George's
River .   .   . Such were the men who under-
took the enterprise, the original fathers of the
present town of Warren."

In 1736 the settlers drew lots for their lots, and
No. 20 fell to WILLIAM[1] McINTYRE. Not long

after, in company with many others, he with-
drew to safer quarters during the Indian massacres. He was for a time master of a sloop.
He was often employed in Boston where several
of his children resided. His son—or more
probably a son-in-law of the same family name,
Neil McIntyre, was established as a tobac-
conist in that city; and Mary, a daughter, was
among the creditors of both WILLIAM[1] and
Robert[2] at their death.

In the "Annals of Warren," Eaton gives the
children of WILLIAM as 1. Robert[2], 2. Neal[2],
3. Capt. John[2], 4. Mary[2]. But in 1906, Mr.
F. P. McIntyre of 197 St. Botolph St., Boston, a
descendant, wrote as follows to Mr. C. K. Bolton, Librarian of the Boston Athenaeum:

"I take pleasure in giving you herewith some
corrections of and some additions to Eaton's
'Annals of Warren' (Maine), concerning
WILLIAM[1] McINTYRE and his sons and daughters. Eaton's 'Annals' was one of the best and
most reliable local histories and genealogies ever
published, and his inaccuracy in this case is
accounted for by the fact that . . . most
of the children of William did not go to St.
George's River, now Warren, Thomaston, and
Cushing, Me."

He then gives it as his opinion that the
children were (order of birth uncertain): 1.
William[2], 2. Robert[2], 3. Martha[2], 4. Esther[2]
(married Neil McIntyre), 5. John[2], 6. Mary[2].
He finds no proof, however, that the first two
are sons of William[1].

Now there is the record of a marriage in Boston on December thirtieth, 1730, of a William McIntyre to Margaret Kirkpatrick. It seems rather probable that this was WILLIAM[1], who had in this country several children born in Ireland (Robert[2], Martha[2], Esther[2], and John[2], but not William[2]), but having lost his first wife married (2) Margaret Kirkpatrick in 1730, and had by her two other children, JOSEPH[2] and Mary[2]. Certain it is that a JOSEPH McINTYRE appears in Georgetown about 1750, who is too old to be the son of Robert[2] or John[2], for in 1756, he marries SARAH[4] WALLIS (SAMUEL[3], JOSIAH[2], JOHN[1]). He is therefore probably the son of the WILLIAM who married MARGARET KIRKPATRICK in 1730, and was born in 1733±. If this hypothesis is correct, JOSEPH was either the son or the grandson of WILLIAM[1]. We incline to the former theory, though perhaps it cannot be proved; but that JOSEPH was in the direct line of WILLIAM[1] seems so probable as almost to amount to a certainty. We shall proceed on the supposition that he is the son of WILLIAM[1].

2. JOSEPH[2] McINTYRE (WILLIAM[1]), of Georgetown, in 1752 signed a petition, with many others, to Lieutenant Governor Phips of Massachusetts, imploring protection. According to the town records his intention of marriage with SARAH[4] WALES (WALLIS) was declared November twelfth, 1756. By the same records they had the following children:

1. Mehitabel[3], born January twenty-second, 1759.
2. Elizabeth[3], born April eighteenth, 1762.
3. Hannah[3], born August twenty-fifth, 1763.
4. Joseph[3], born April twelfth, 1767.
5. Nancy[3], born November fifteenth, 1768.
6. William[3], born September seventeenth, 1770.

But evidence has been found of two more children, not upon these records: RACHEL[3], who was married in 1789, and Henry[3], who was a minor in 1776. Evidently one of these was born about 1765, and the other about 1772. Probably RACHEL[1] was the older.

JOSEPH[2] McINTYRE died in 1776, and his widow was appointed administratrix. His property was inventoried at seven hundred and eight pounds. Mention is made of three minor sons, Joseph, William, and Henry.

3. RACHEL[3] McINTYRE (JOSEPH[2], WILLIAM[1]) was born in Georgetown in 1765± or 1772±; probably the former. On October thirty-first, 1789, she was published, and on December seventeenth 1789 married by Rev. Ezekiel Emerson to WILLIAM[6] SPRAGUE (LIEUTENANT WILLIAM[5], JETHRO[4], WILLIAM[3], JOHN[2], FRANCIS[1]) of the same place (see SPRAGUE family).

By the marriage of RACHEL[3] McINTYRE, in 1789,
    the name of McINTYRE was merged in that of SPRAGUE, in 1812
    the name of SPRAGUE was merged in that of HOPKINS, in 1847
    the name of HOPKINS was merged in that of MUNSEY.

AUTHORITIES

1. "Registry of Deeds, Lincoln Co., Maine," 49:132-134.
2. Lincoln County "Probate Records."
3. Certified copy of Georgetown, Maine, Town Records.
4. Copy of letter from F. P. McIntyre.
5. Eaton's "Annals of Warren."
6. Letter from H. C. Thayer.
7. Georgetown "Vital Records."
8. "History of Bristol and Bremen."
9. *Maine Historical Society Collections*, 6:18ff.

THE MAYO FAMILY

1. REV. JOHN[1] MAYO came from England to Barnstable in 1639. He taught there in Rev. John Lathrop's church till 1644, when he removed to Eastham. He took charge of a church there from 1646 to 1655, when he was settled over the Second Church in Boston. This was the North Church in North Square. The pastor's residence was at what is now 298 Hanover Street. He remained there from 1655 to 1673 when he retired because of old age. His colleague and successor was the Rev. Increase Mather. REVEREND MR. MAYO went from Boston to Yarmouth, where he spent the remaining years of his life with his daughter Elizabeth. He died at Yarmouth in May, 1676. His wife's name was THOMASINE (TAMSIN); her maiden name is not known. She died February twenty-sixth, 1682/3. Their children, all born before 1639, were:

1. SAMUEL[2]   2. Hannah[2]   3. Nathaniel[2]
4. John[2]   5. Elizabeth[2]

2. CAPTAIN SAMUEL[2] MAYO (REV. JOHN[1]), of

Barnstable, Oyster Bay (Long Island), and Boston, was born in England in 1620±. He seems to have come with his father to Barnstable, and for many years resided there. In 1643 he married TAMSIN[2] LUMPKIN (WILLIAM[1]) of Yarmouth, who was born in 1626. In 1653, he, with Peter Wright and Rev. William Leveridge, of Sandwich, were purchasers of Oyster Bay on Long Island. The year after, in company with others, he removed thither. In 1654, he was pressed into an expedition against the Dutch. He is then spoken of as "of Barnstable," perhaps because he had not gained a residence in his new home. How long he was detained in service is not certain; but in 1658 he moved to Boston, where he died, in middle life, in 1663. In April, 1664, power of administration was granted to his father, REV. JOHN[1] MAYO on the estate of SAMUEL[2] MAYO, deceased, mariner,—his widow, THOMASINE, declining to administer. MRS. SAMUEL[1] MAYO afterwards married Mr. John Sunderland of Eastham (born 1618). She died in her eighty-fourth year, June sixteenth, 1709, and was buried in the old burying ground in Harwich (now Brewster). Mr. John Sunderland died December twenty-sixth, 1703, in his eighty-fifth year; his first wife died January twenty-ninth, 1663.

The children of CAPTAIN SAMUEL[2] and TAMSIN (LUMPKIN) MAYO were:

1. Mary[3]	2. Samuel[3]	3. Hannah[3]
4. ELIZABETH[3]	5. Joseph[3]	6. John[3]
7. Nathaniel[3]	8. SARAH[3]	

3.1. ELIZABETH[3] MAYO (CAPTAIN SAMUEL[2], REV. JOHN[1]) was baptized May twenty-second, 1653, in Boston. On May sixteenth, 1674, she married REV. SAMUEL[3] TREAT (GOVERNOR ROBERT[2], RICHARD[1]), her father's successor in the Eastham pulpit (see TREAT family). Sewall refers to her marriage in his diary. She died December fourth, 1696.

By the marriage of ELIZABETH[3] MAYO, in 1674,
the name of MAYO   was merged in that of TREAT; in 1694
the name of TREAT   was merged in that of FREEMAN II,
in 1719
the name of FREEMAN II   was merged in that of HOPKINS,
and in 1847
the name of HOPKINS   was merged in that of MUNSEY.

3.2. SARAH[3] MAYO (CAPTAIN SAMUEL[2], REV. JOHN[1]), was born in 1660. She married LIEUTENANT EDMUND[3] FREEMAN (see FREEMAN I family), being probably his second wife. She died in 1745.

By the marriage of SARAH[3] MAYO, sister of ELIZABETH[3] MAYO,
the name of MAYO   was merged in that of FREEMAN I,
in 1717
the name of FREEMAN I   was merged in that of COBB, in 1755
the name of COBB   was merged in that of HOPKINS;
and in 1847
the name of HOPKINS   was merged in that of MUNSEY.

AUTHORITIES

1. Treat Genealogy.
2. Mayo Genealogy (MS in Hist.-Gen. Library, Boston).
3. *N. E. Historical and Genealogical Register*, Vol. 6.
4. Freeman Genealogy.
5. Suffolk Probate Record, 4:197.

THE MEREEN FAMILY

1. LIEUTENANT JOHN[1] MEREEN, of Eastham, Massachusetts, and Georgetown, Maine, married October twenty-second, 1754, REBECCA[4] PEPPER (JOSEPH[3], ISAAC[2], ROBERT[1]), also of Eastham. There is a persistent tradition among the Mereens that they are of French origin. This tradition has been handed down from father to son ever since the days of JOHN[1]. Doubtless it is true. But it also is likely that the name has been greatly modified from the original. We know that when from 1662 to 1680 refugees from France and the Channel Islands found asylum among us, Jean Le Brun became plain "John Brown"; Philippe L'Anglois, "Philip English"; and François Gerneaux, "Frank Gano." Possibly the French original of Mereen was Marigny, for Pierre Berthon de Marigny was leader of the Narragansett Colony of Huguenots in Rhode Island from 1681 to 1685. This theory becomes plausible when we note that when JOHN[1] MEREEN's intention of marriage was entered upon the Eastham Records, the clerk spelled his surname "Merign"; while in the marriage record the same man is called "Mareen." Spelling followed the lines of least resistance in those days.

Another possibility is, that the ancestors of John were French *marines*. Weiss, in his "History of the Protestant Refugees," states that, after the revocation of the Edict of Nantes

(1685), "a great number of soldiers and officers of the *marine* abandoned the French service for that of Holland," and that "many fugitives were engaged as officers or *marine* volunteers." The running title on page fifty-one of the volume quoted is "French *Marines* in Holland." Now we know that many Huguenots fled hither in the latter part of the seventeenth century. May there not have been *French Marines* in America as well?

John[1] MEREEN was a *mariner*, at any rate. His great granddaughter (now living [in 1906]), states that her grandfather has often told her how his father was captain of a vessel which was wrecked on Cape Cod. The son, John[2], then a boy of twelve, was with him. He, too, became a mariner and was shipmaster for many years. He gave up following the sea because of lameness, and for thirty-five years was collector and treasurer of the town of Phippsburg, Maine.

But CAPTAIN JOHN[1] was more than a *marine*. When the Revolutionary War broke out, he left the sea and took up arms upon the land. In 1779 we find him enrolled as Second Lieutenant in Capt. Benjamin Lamont's (9th) Company of Col. Sam. McCobb's (Lincoln County) Regiment. His name has now evolved into MEREEN.

Just when LIEUTENANT JOHN[1] (as we shall now call him) left Cape Cod is not known. His grandson, John Flavel[3] Mereen, a prominent citizen of Phippsburg, who died in 1883, used to say that his grandfather sold his farm on the Cape for nine hundred dollars in continental money and came to buy land at Basin Point, Phippsburg—then Georgetown. Meanwhile his money proved worthless and he lost everything; but he settled there all the same. The dates of his discharge from the army and of his death are unknown.

The children of LIEUTENANT JOHN[1] and REBECCA[4] (PEPPER) MEREEN were:

1. REBECCA[2]   2. Ruth[2]   3. Hannah[2]
4. Samuel[2]   5. Daniel[2]   6. John[2]
7. Sarah[2]

2. REBECCA[2] MEREEN (LIEUTENANT JOHN[1]) was born in Eastham, September thirteenth, 1762. According to the Harpswell town records, she married ELISHA[6] HOPKINS (SIMEON[5], CALEB[4-3], GILES[2], STEPHEN[1]) of Harpswell, Maine, on May sixteenth, 1784 (see HOPKINS LINE).

By the marriage of REBECCA[3] MEREEN, in 1784, the name of MEREEN was merged in that of HOPKINS; in 1847 the name of HOPKINS was merged in that of MUNSEY.

AUTHORITIES

1. Weiss, "History of the French Protestant Refugees."
2. Eastham Records.
3. Harpswell Records.
4. Revolutionary Lists.
5. Letters from several great-grandchildren.

THE MERRITT FAMILY

1. HENRY[1] MERRITT was born in the county of Kent, England, about 1590. He was one of the earliest settlers of Scituate and became a large landed proprietor. He was made a freeman in 1638. He died intestate in November, 1653. His wife's name is unknown; some say it was Deborah.

His children:

   1. JOHN[2]   2. Henry[2]   3. CATHERINE[2]

2.1. JOHN[2] MERRITT (HENRY[1]), of Scituate, was born in 1625±. He administered his father's estate in 1653. On April third, 1655, he was married by Captain Humphrey Atherton, of Cambridge, to ELIZABETH[2] WYBORNE (THOMAS[1]) of Boston (see WYBORNE family). In the days of the English Commonwealth only *civil* marriages were legal. JOHN[2] lived on the paternal homestead, but died in middle life (1676), leaving three sons:

   1. JOHN[3]   2. Henry[3]   3. Jonathan[3]

2.2. CATHERINE[2] MERRITT (HENRY[1]), of Scituate was married in 1644 to JOHN[1] DAMON.

> By the marriage of CATHERINE[2] MERRITT, in 1644, the name of MERRITT was merged in that of DAMON, but in 1727 the name of DAMON was merged in that of MERRITT (see below, JONATHAN[4] MERRITT).

3. JOHN[3] MERRITT (JOHN[2], HENRY[1]) of Scituate was born in 1660. He married in 1686 ELIZABETH[3]

HYLAND (THOMAS², THOMAS¹) (see HYLAND family) and became the father of twelve children:

1. John⁴	2. Thomas⁴	3. Elizabeth⁴
4. Mary⁴	5. Ichabod⁴	6. Hannah⁴
7. Henry⁴	8. Abigail⁴	9. JONATHAN⁴
10 David⁴	11. Ebenezer⁴	12. Ezekiel⁴

4. JONATHAN⁴ MERRITT (JOHN³⁻², HENRY¹), of Scituate, Massachusetts, and Hebron, Connecticut, was born in 1702, at Scituate. On January eighth, 1727, he married a townswoman, MEHITABLE³ DAMON (LIEUTENANT ZACHARY², JOHN¹), granddaughter of CATHERINE² MERRITT, the sister of JONATHAN⁴ MERRITT's grandfather (see DAMON family). Stearns ("History of Ashburnham") calls MEHITABLE² the granddaughter of LIEUTENANT ZACHARY², but the Vital Records of Scituate show that Mehitable⁴ was too young to marry in 1727. About 1730, JONATHAN⁴ removed from Scituate, finally settling in Hebron, Connecticut, where he died October twenty-first, 1758. Only three children are mentioned:

1. Simeon⁵   2. NOAH⁵   3. Jonathan⁵

5. NOAH⁵ MERRITT (JONATHAN⁴, JOHN³⁻², HENRY¹), is said by Stearns to have been born in 1730, though his name does not appear in the Scituate Vital Records. As his father moved about this time to Connecticut, he may first have seen the light in that state. He married SARAH³ LEE (ISAAC², SAMUEL¹) of Watertown. Stearns says he can find no record of his marriage, and many genealogists searched in vain for it for twenty

years. We have finally unearthed it among
the Thompson (formerly Killingly), Connecticut, church records, as follows:

"NOAH MERRITT married April 12, 1759,
SARAH LEE."

Previous to his marriage he is found in Templeton, Massachusetts (1753); but he was a soldier
in the French and Indian War in 1755, in Colonel Eliphalet Dyer's Third Connecticut Regiment. He settled in Templeton, and raised a
family of thirteen children:

1. Noah[6]	2. Abigail[6]	3. Lucy[6]
4. Sarah[6]	5. Henry[6]	6. Esther[6]
7. Simeon[6]	8. Molly[6]	9 Eunice[6]
10. Wilks[6]	11. Uriah[6]	12. Hannah[6]

13. Dytha[8] (which seems to be a misprint for *Lydia*).

6. Lucy[6] Merritt (Noah[5], Jonathan[4], John[3-2],
Henry[1]), of Templeton, Massachusetts, was
born May twenty-fifth, 1762. On July third,
1786, she married George[5] Sawyer (Aholiab[4],
William[3], Thomas[2-1]) of Bolton (see Sawyer
family).

By the marriage of Lucy[6] Merritt, in 1786,
the name of Merritt was merged in that of Sawyer; in 1812
the name of Sawyer was merged in that of Munsey.

AUTHORITIES

1. *N. E. Historical and Genealogical Register*, Vols. 19, 33.
2. Deane's "Scituate."
3. Scituate Vital Records.
4. Templeton Vital Records.
5. Killingly (Thompson), Connecticut, Church Records.
6. *Mayflower Descendant*, Vols. 1, 2, 9, 11.
7. *Boston Transcript*, 1898, 1902.
8. "Ninth Report of Record Commissioners" of Boston.
9. Stearns's "History of Ashburnham."
10. Connecticut Historic Society Collections, Vol. IX.
   French and Indian War Rolls, 1:37.

THE MULLINS FAMILY

1. WILLIAM[1] MULLINS (MOLINES, MUL-
   LENS), with his wife ALICE, joined the Pilgrims at Southampton, England. With them
   were a son JOSEPH and a daughter PRIS-
   CILLA. They left in England a son William
   and a married daughter, Sarah (Mullins) Blun-
   den. WILLIAM[1] "was one of the most efficient
   of the organizers and managers of the colony."
   He was one of the forty-one signers of the immortal Compact on board the *Mayflower* (see
   BREWSTER family).

   Recent investigations have shown that he
   came from Dorking, in Surrey, near London.
   He was a tradesman by occupation and one
   of the seventy (more or less) famous Merchant
   Adventurers whose aim was "to do good and to
   plant religion" (Noble's "Pilgrims," page 158).
   Of the seven thousand pounds invested in their
   enterprise, WILLIAM[1] MULLINS is said to
   have contributed five hundred pounds. But
   his career was brief. In a little more than two
   months after reaching Plymouth, he passed
   away. He made a nuncupative will to GOVER-
   NOR CARVER February twenty-first, 1620,
   and then closed his eyes in death. The will is
   given in the *Mayflower Descendant* (1:230). In
   this will the name is spelled MULLENS.

   ALICE MULLINS did not long survive her
   husband. The strain of that awful first winter
   proved too much for her constitution. BRAD-

FORD writes: "Mr. MOLINES, and his WIFE, his SONE, and his servant [ROBERT CAR-TER], dyed the first winter.   Only his daughter, PRISCILLA survived, and maried with JOHN ALDEN" ("History of Plimoth," page 536). There is some indication that WILLIAM¹ was a lineal descendant of Edward I of England.

The children of WILLIAM¹ and ALICE MULLINS were:

1. William²   2. Sarah²   3. PRISCILLA²   4. JOSEPH²

2. PRISCILLA² MULLINS (WILLIAM¹), one of the *Mayflower* passengers, was born in England.   By the death of her parents, early in 1621, she was left a double orphan.   How CAPTAIN MILES STANDISH loved the fair maiden, and how he sent to her as his envoy JOHN¹ ALDEN (see ALDEN family) with unlooked-for results, has been related by Henry W. Longfellow, who was one of PRISCILLA'S descendants.

As he warmed and glowed, in his simple and eloquent language.
Quite forgetful of self, and full of the praise of his rival,
Archly the maiden smiled, and, with eyes overrunning with laughter,
Said, in a tremulous voice: "Why don't you speak for yourself, John?"

By the marriage of PRISCILLA² MULLINS, in 1622,
   the name of MULLINS was merged in that of ALDEN; in 1644
   the name of ALDEN was merged in that of PAYBODY; in 1683
   the name of PAYBODY was merged in that of BARTLETT, in 1738
   the name of BARTLETT was merged in that of SPRAGUE, in 1812
   the name of SPRAGUE was merged in that of HOPKINS; in 1847
   the name of HOPKINS was merged in that of MUNSEY.

AUTHORITIES

1. *Mayflower Descendant*, Vol. 1.
2. "Eliab Alden."
3. *Boston Transcript*, 1892, 1911.
4. *N. E. Historical and Genealogical Register*, Vol. 42.
5. Bradford's "History of Plymouth."
6. "Peabody Genealogy."
7. Noble's (F. A.) "Pilgrims."

THE PEABODY FAMILY

1. JOHN[1] PAYBODY (PAYBODIE, PEABODY), of England, came to Plymouth, Massachusetts, as early as 1636, for he was admitted freeman in that year. He received a grant of land (ten acres) in 1637/8. He was a member of a jury which convicted three young Englishmen of the murder of an Indian, September fourth, 1638; was on "the Grand Inquest" of June fourth, 1639; and was surety on a neighbor's bond in 1645. He made his will July sixteenth, 1649, naming his wife ISABEL, three sons, and a daughter therein. There is no existing record of his death, though it probably has occurred. His children were:

    1. Thomas[2]   2. Francis[2]   3. WILLIAM[2]   4. Annis[2]

2. WILLIAM[2] PAYBODY (JOHN[1]), of Duxbury, was born in England in 1620±. He grew up in Duxbury with his father, and then made a position and acquired a competency for himself. He bore arms in CAPTAIN STANDISH'S Duxbury Company in 1643. He was a "yeoman", (1648), a "boatman" and "planter" (1672), and

a "wheelwright" (1681). He was also a land surveyor, for many years the town clerk, and a Representative to the General Court from 1654 to 1663, again in 1668, and from 1671 to 1682. He was admitted freeman in 1651. He made his will May thirteenth, 1707, and died at Little Compton (now in Rhode Island) December thirteenth, 1707. He married, December twenty-sixth, 1644, ELIZABETH[2], eldest daughter of JOHN[1] and PRISCILLA[2] (MULLINS) ALDEN (see ALDEN family). His children, whose births he entered with his own hand upon records which still exist, were:

1. John[3]	2. Elizabeth[3]	3. Mary[3]
4. Mercy[3]	5. Martha[3]	6. Priscilla[3]
7. Priscilla 2d[3]	8. Sarah[3]	9. Ruth[3]
10. Rebecca[3]	11. HANNAH[3]	12. William[3]
13. Lydia[3]		

3. HANNAH[3] PAYBODY (WILLIAM[2], JOHN[1]), of Duxbury, was born October fifteenth, 1662. On October second, 1683, she married SAMUEL[3] BARTLETT (BENJAMIN[2], ROBERT[1]), of the same town (see BARTLETT family).

By the marriage of HANNAH[3] PAYBODY, in 1683, the name of PAYBODY was merged in that of BARTLETT; in 1738 the name of BARTLETT was merged in that of SPRAGUE; in 1812 the name of SPRAGUE was merged in that of HOPKINS; in 1847 the name of HOPKINS was merged in that of MUNSEY.

AUTHORITIES

1. *Mayflower Descendant*, Vols. 1, 6.
2. "Year Book" (1897-98), Society of Colonial Wars.
3. "Peabody Genealogy."
4. Austen's "Genealogical Dictionary."

THE PEPPERRELL FAMILY

1. COLONEL WILLIAM[1] PEPPERRELL (or PEPPER-
ELL) (1647-1734), was the first of his name to
come to America. He was born at Tavistock,
near Plymouth, England. At the age of twenty-
two he came to this country in a fishing schooner,
and settled at the Isle of Shoals; six years later
he removed to Kittery, where he engaged in
shipbuilding along with JOHN[1] BRAY, the pioneer
shipbuilder of the town. After a courtship of
three years he married MR. BRAY's daughter,
MARGERY[2], who was but nineteen (see BRAY
family). MR. BRAY at first hesitated to let his
daughter wed with a man of slender means;
but young PEPPERRELL's business capacity soon
won him over. Not many years later MR.
PEPPERRELL had a fleet of more than one hundred fishing schooners on the Grand Banks of
Newfoundland, besides others engaged in foreign trade. JOHN[1] BRAY presented his son-in-
law with a house lot at Kittery, on which WIL-
LIAM[1] PEPPERRELL erected a house which is still
standing.

COLONEL PEPPERRELL became Justice of the
Peace in 1690, and held the office for thirty-five
years. He was appointed Judge of the Court
of Common Pleas in 1715, and served in that
capacity for many years with his son William[2]
as clerk. His business prospered, and in 1717,
he took his son into partnership in shipping,
lumber, and fisheries. He was one of the ori-

ginal founders of the Congregational Church of
Kittery, and ever an active member. His ver-
satility is shown by the fact that he was not only
an enterprising merchant, a distinguished jurist,
and a zealous churchman, but he also won renown in those troublous times as a soldier. He
commanded the garrison at Kittery Point during
an Indian uprising in a fort named after himself,
and for his services there and elsewhere rose to
the rank of Lieutenant-Colonel. On the family
tomb is this inscription:

"Here lyes the body of the Honorable WIL-
LIAM PEPPEREL, ESQ., who departed this life
the 15th of February Anno Domini 1733, in the
87th year of his age, with the remains of great
part of his family."

MRS. MARGERY[2] (BRAY) PEPPERRELL, died
April twenty-fourth, 1741. Her historian speaks
of her as "exemplary for unaffected piety and
amiable virtue—especially her charity, her courteous affability, her prudence, meekness, patience, and unweariedness in well-doing."

COLONEL PEPPERRELL and his wife had eight
children, two sons and six daughters:

1. Andrew[2]	2. Mary[2]	3. Margery[2]
4. JOANNA[2]	5. Miriam[2]	6. William[2]
7. Dorothy[2]	8. Jane[2]	

Of these eight children the sixth became famous. He was a successful merchant and jurist,
like his father; but in military skill and renown he
far surpassed him. He was given command of
the British land forces in 1745, and led the suc-

cessful expedition which resulted in the capture of Lewisburg. As a reward for this achievement he was knighted by the king of England, and had the unique distinction of being the only native American that was ever made a baronet. He passed a year in England, and on his return lived in truly English fashion. "His walls were hung with costly mirrors and paintings, his sideboards loaded with silver, his cellars filled with choice wines, his park stocked with deer, a retinue of servants, a splendid barge with a black crew dressed in uniform, and all maintained in Baronial style." A fine portrait of the Baronet hangs in the rotunda of the Capitol at Augusta, Maine.

The brothers and sisters of Sir William[2] Pepperrell seem to have been more democratic. We are especially interested in:

2. JOANNA[2] PEPPERRELL (COLONEL WILLIAM[1]), who was born in Kittery, June twenty-second, 1692; on March twentieth, 1710/11, she married DR. GEORGE[2] JACKSON (DR. GEORGE[1] of Marblehead: see ABORN and JACKSON families) of Kittery. A notice of her death is found in Willis's *Old Eliot* (IV, 46), a part of which is as follows:

Kittery, Feb. 17, 1725/6. This Day Expir'd MRS. JOANNA JACKSON, in the 34th year of her age: the late Excellent Consort of MR. GEORGE JACKSON, Physician [*sic*] by whom she had 7 children, and Daughter of LIEUT. COL. PEPPERRELL, Esq.: and MARGERY his Wife:
She was a Comely Person, but her Principal Ornaments were the Virtues of her Mind. She was Exemplary in her whole Conversation towards all her Relatives; was Beneficial to all, especially to the Living Images of God;

Manifested more than ordinary Compassion to Sick People, and was forward to Relieve the Poor.

The children of Joanna[2] (Pepperrell) and Dr. George[2] Jackson were:

1. Margery[3]   2. Mary[3]   3. Elizabeth[3]
4. Joanna[3]   5. Dorothy[3]   6. Jane[3]
7. Miriam[3]   8. Sarah[3], died in infancy

The fifth child, Dorothy[3] Jackson (born November twenty-first, 1717) was the grandmother of Andrew[5] Munsey. She married Derry[3] Pitman (Nathaniel[2], William[1]) in 1736 (see Pitman family); their daughter Mary[4] Pitman (born 1749) married Timothy[4] Munsey in 1772 (see Munsey Line), and their son Andrew[5] Munsey was born in 1785.

By the marriage of Joanna[2] Pepperrell, in 1711,
    the name of Pepperrell was merged in that of Jackson; in 1736 the name of Jackson was merged in that of Pitman; in 1772* the name of Pitman was merged in that of MUNSEY.

The *New England Magazine* (12:415) says: "The Pepperrell Family as such is found in this country for only about seventy-five years. During that period they amassed the largest fortune ever known at that time in New England, receiving the greatest honors ever conferred on a colonial by the mother country."

AUTHORITIES

1. *New England Family History*, Vol. I.
2. Willis's *Old Eliot*, Vol IV.

*There was also an earlier Pitman-Munsey merger; see Mary[3] Aborn, page 51.

3. Stackpole's "Old Kittery."
4. Parsons's "Life of Sir Wm. Pepperrell."
5. *New England Magazine*, Vol. XII.
6. Belknap's "History of New Hampshire."
7. "Year Book" (1895), Society of Colonial Wars.

THE PITMAN FAMILY

1. WILLIAM[1] PITMAN (1632-1682) seems to have been at Plymouth for a time in his youth; but he soon removed to Boston, where, November twenty-ninth, 1653, he was married to Barbara Evans by William Hibbins.* By 1657 he was living at Oyster River (now Durham, formerly part of Dover), New Hampshire, where he was taxed as late as 1677. His eldest son was born in 1658. His will was proved in 1682. He left the following children, most of them by a second wife, ANNE ———, whom he married as early as 1665:

i. John[2]	ii. Francis[2]	iii. Ezekiel[2]
iv. NATHANIEL[2]	v. JOSEPH[2]	vi. Elizabeth[2]
vii. Abigail[2]	viii. Sarah[2]	ix. Anne[2]
x. Zachariah[2]	xi. Hannah[2]	xii. Judith[2]

2(iv) NATHANIEL[2] PITMAN (WILLIAM[1]) of Oyster River, New Hampshire, received a grant of thirty acres of land June twenty-third, 1701. He married MRS. DELIVERANCE (———) DERRY, the widow of John Derry, before September twenty-second, 1701—probably in 1697. John and DELIVERANCE had been taken captive by

---

*See footnote on page 63.

the Indians in the Oyster River massacre of
1694. The husband and a child, John, Jr., died
in captivity. NATHANIEL[2] PITMAN must have
died before 1738, for on August third of that
year, Mrs. DELIVERANCE is again a widow, and
sells sixty acres of land to her son DERRY[3], on
condition that he shall give her an honorable
burial after her decease, and pay twenty pounds
to each of her sisters. The children of NATHA-
NIEL[2] PITMAN, so far as known, were:

1. DERRY[3]   2. Tabitha[3]   3. Abigail[3]

3(iv) DERRY[3] PITMAN (NATHANIEL[2], WILLIAM[1]), of
Dover, was born at Oyster River in 1698.
Early in 1736 he married DOROTHY[3] JACKSON
(DR. GEORGE[2], DR. GEORGE[1]) (see JACKSON
family). He joined the Dover church May
twenty-fourth, 1724; his wife joined November
fourteenth, 1756. He was mentioned in the will
of Sir William[2] Pepperrell in 1759. He lived
later in Madbury and Durham. On May
twelfth, 1761, DERRY[3] PITMAN of Durham, inn-
holder, and DOROTHY[3] his wife sold their fifth
interest in the estate of DR. GEORGE[2] JACKSON,
late of Salem, to one Jeremiah Lee of Marblehead. The last mention of DERRY[3] PITMAN
that has been found on record is in a deed dated
1764, which gives his residence as Durham. In
the Durham records twin children are mentioned:

1. Andrew Pepperrell[4]   2. MARY[4]

4(iv) MARY[4] PITMAN (DERRY[3], NATHANIEL[2], WIL-

LIAM[1]) was born in Durham, New Hampshire, March twenty-second, 1749. She was, as we have seen, a twin with Andrew Pepperrell[4] Pitman. In 1772 she married TIMOTHY[4] MUNSEY (See MUNSEY LINE).

2(v) JOSEPH[2] PITMAN (WILLIAM[1]). Very little is known of JOSEPH[2] PITMAN, except that he was the son of WILLIAM[1] and the father of ZACHARIAH[3]. According to Savage, he was bound to William Tasket in 1686, apparently as an apprentice, but was discharged by the court because of the cruelty of his master. He was killed by the Indians August nineteenth, 1704. He is merely a connecting link, but as such is valuable.

3(v) ZACHARIAH[3] PITMAN (JOSEPH[2], WILLIAM[1]) of Madbury, New Hampshire, was married to MERCY[2] CONNER (TIMOTHY[1]) November thirteenth, 1723, by Rev. Jeremiah Wise, of Dover. He headed a petition May tenth, 1743; was one of the petitioners for the incorporation of Madbury in 1758. In his will of June third, 1783 (Strafford County Probate Records, 2:153) he says: "I will and bequeath unto my daughter, ABIGAIL MUNSEY, wife of DAVID MUNSEY, one cow, etc."

4(v) ABIGAIL[4] PITMAN (ZACHARIAH[3], JOSEPH[2], WILLIAM[1]) of Madbury was baptized by Rev. J. Cushing of Dover in 1728. She married DAVID[3] MUNSEY (also baptized 1728, when about seven years old*), as shown above, some time before

---

*See page 13, DAVID[3] MUNSEY.

1749. Her son TIMOTHY[4] MUNSEY married MARY[4] PITMAN (DERRY[3], NATHANIEL[2], WILLIAM[1]). Thus two lines of WILLIAM[1] PITMAN'S descendants were merged in the MUNSEY line.

AUTHORITIES

1. *N. E. Historical and Genealogical Register*, Vols. 7, 9, 10, 23,30, 33.
2. "Wentworth Genealogy."
3. "Thurston and Pitman Families" (C. M. Thurston).
4. Quint's "First Parish, Dover."
5. Coverley's "Annals of Boodeys."
6. Rev. Hugh Adams's "Records—Oyster River."
7. Dover "Historic Collections."
8. Teale's "Historical Memories of Ancient Dover."
9. "Landmarks in Ancient Dover."
10. New Hampshire *Historic Collections*, Vol. 8.
11. Strafford County "Probate Records," Vol. 2.
12. "Ninth Report of Record Commissioners of Boston."
13. Goodwin's "Pilgrim Republic."
14. *Essex Antiquarian*, Vol. 3.
15. New Hampshire "State Papers," XXXI. 260.
16. "Dover (New Hampshire), Marriages," by J. R. Ham, page 167.

THE PRESCOTT FAMILY

1. JOHN[1] PRESCOTT, the founder of Lancaster, Massachusetts, was born in Standish, England, in 1604. He married MARY PLATTS at Wygan, Lancashire, January twenty-first, 1629; he died in America in 1683. He left England to avoid persecution. In 1638 he landed at Barbadoes, where he bought land. In 1640 he came to New England and settled in Watertown.

In 1643, with Thomas King and others, he purchased "Nashaway" (a part of which is now
Lancaster), and became one of the earliest
settlers. Nourse, in his "Annals of Lancaster,"
says the town would have been named "Prescott" had its founder been a freeman*; but he
had never given public adhesion to the established church covenant, and was therefore in-
capable of voting or holding office. In 1669,
however, he was admitted freeman. He was a
farmer, blacksmith, and millwright.

JOHN[1] PRESCOTT was a heroic figure in the
early history of Lancaster and Groton. He
brought with him a metallic coat of mail, which
he sometimes wore when dealing with the sa-
vages; this served to impress them, as his force,
capacity, and judgment did his white neighbors. Nourse calls him an "ideal pioneer,"
a "true builder of the nation." He distinguished himself for bravery and leadership in
the Indian Wars. He served in the garrison at
Lancaster, and in the defense of the town
against the Indians on August twenty-second,
1675, and February tenth, 1676.

He had a numerous family of descendants,
many of whom have been persons of great ability
and distinction. His great-grandson, Colonel
William Prescott, was chief in command at the
Battle of Bunker Hill. Another descendant was
William H. Prescott, the famous historian of the

* See footnote on page 50.

"Conquest of Mexico," "Conquest of Peru,"
etc. At the time of his death, in 1683, his family
had become one of the wealthiest and most in-
fluential in Massachusetts.

JOHN[1] and MARY[1] (PLATT(s)) PRESCOTT had
eight children:

1. MARY[2]	2. Martha[2]	3. John[2]
4. Sarah[2]	5. Hannah[2]	6. Lydia[2]
7. Jonathan[2]	8. Jonas[2]	

2. MARY[2] PRESCOTT (JOHN[1]) was born in England.
She was baptized in Halifax Parish, February
twenty-fourth, 1630/1. At the age of eighteen
she married THOMAS[1] SAWYER of Lancaster (see
SAWYER family), and by him became the mother
of eleven children. She survived her husband,
who died on September twelfth, 1706.

By the marriage of MARY[2] PRESCOTT, in 1648,
the name of PRESCOTT　was merged in that of SAWYER,
and in 1812
the name of SAWYER　was merged in that of **MUNSEY.**

AUTHORITIES

1. Society of Colonial Wars, "Illinois, 1900."
2. Nourse's "Annals of Lancaster."

THE PRINCE FAMILY

1. GOVERNOR THOMAS[1] PRENCE ("PRINCE", we
style it, but he wrote it PRENCE) of Plymouth,
Duxbury, and Eastham, was born 1600± in the
parish of Lechlade, Gloucestershire, England.
He was the son of Thomas Prence of All Saints
Barking, London, a carriage maker. THOMAS[1]
came to Plymouth, Mass., in the *Fortune*, in

1621. Soon he became recognized as a member of ELDER BREWSTER'S family, and on August fifth, 1624, he married the Elder's daughter, PATIENCE[2]. This was the ninth marriage in the colony.

In July, 1627, MR. PRENCE[1], and a half dozen of the most prominent of the colonists, agreed to assume all debts (about two thousand four hundred pounds) and conduct the entire trade. The main purpose of this was to devise means to bring over more of their friends from Leyden. In this they were successful.

In 1634 PRENCE'S FIRST WIFE died. In that year he was elected Governor for the first time. Later he removed from Plymouth to Duxbury, which prevented his immediate re-election, since there was a requirement that the governor should live at Plymouth. Accordingly he was chosen Assistant; but in 1638 he was again elected Governor and allowed to reside in Duxbury. After a short time he was succeeded by WILLIAM BRADFORD, who died in 1657. Then PRENCE[1] was elected for the third time, and held office until his death in 1673.

He was married four times: (1) to PATIENCE[2] BREWSTER in 1624; (2) to Mary Collier (WILLIAM[1]) in 1635; (3) to MRS. APPHIA, widow of SAMUEL[1] FREEMAN, before December eighth, 1662; and (4) to Mrs. Mary, widow of Thomas[1] Howes.

He died at Eastham, March twenty-ninth, 1673; he was buried at Plymouth.

His children were:

1. Thomas[2]	2. Rebecca[2]	3. Mary[2]
4. MERCY[2]	5. Elizabeth[2]	6. Judith[2]
7. Hannah[2]	8. Jane[2]	9. Sarah[2]

The eulogies pronounced upon GOVERNOR PRENCE by his friends at the time [of his death and by succeeding generations are remarkable. The Plymouth Church records speak of his departure (although he lived to the ripe age of seventy-three) as "a very awfull frowne of God upon this chh & colony." Cotton Mather spoke at great length upon his virtues and accomplishments. In the course of this tribute he says:

Sometimes during the life, but always after the death of GOV. BRADFORD, even until his own, MR. THOMAS PRENCE was chosen Governor of Plymouth. He was a man where natural parts exceeded his acquired; but the want and worth of acquired parts was a thing so sensible to him, that Plymouth never had a greater Mecaenas of learning in it. It was he that in spite of much contradiction procured revenues for the support of grammar schools in that colony . . He ever would refuse anything that looked like a bribe; so if any person having a case to be heard at Court had sent a present unto his family in his absence, he would presently send back the value thereof in money unto the person. Had he been only a private Christian [he manifested] a strict walk with God, which might justly have been made an example to the whole colony.

2. MERCY[2] PRENCE (GOVERNOR THOMAS[1]) was born in Plymouth in 1631. On February thirteenth, 1649/50, she married MAJOR JOHN[2] FREEMAN (EDMUND[1]) of Sandwich (see FREEMAN Ifamily).

By the marriage of MERCY[2] PRENCE, in 1649/50,

the name of PRENCE was merged in that of FREEMAN I;
in 1717
the name of FREEMAN I was merged in that of COBB;
in 1755
the name of COBB was merged in that of HOPKINS,
and in 1847
the name of HOPKINS was merged in that of **MUNSEY.**

AUTHORITIES

1. Pope's "Pioneers of Massachusetts."
2. Plymouth "Court Orders."
3. *Mayflower Descendant*, Vols. 1, 4, 6.
4. *New England Family History*, Vol. 2.
5. Cotton Mather's "Magnalia," II, ii, 2.
6. Society of Colonial Wars, "Year Book," (1894).

THE SAWYER FAMILY

1. THOMAS[1] SAWYER, of Rowley and Lancaster, Massachusetts, was born in England about 1616. His father's name is said to have been JOHN. Thomas was one of "three brothers" (Thomas, Edward, and William) who came to Massachusetts after 1640. Thomas and Edward were at Rowley in 1643; in 1647 Thomas went to Lancaster. This is the oldest town in Worcester County; it was incorporated in 1653, but from 1676 to 1681 it was abandoned as unsafe, owing to Indian incursions during King Philip's War. THOMAS[1] SAWYER was one of the first six settlers, and one of the Prudential Managers and Dividers of Land. In 1648 he married MARY[2] PRESCOTT, daughter of JOHN[1] PRESCOTT, the head man of the settlement; she was baptized at Sowerby, England, February twenty-fourth, 1630/1.

THOMAS[1] SAWYER lived next south of his father-in-law, at Lancaster, on ground "recently [1884] occupied by the Seventh Day Advent Society, and now the residence of his descendant, Sally (Sawyer) Chase." He took part in King Philip's War, a garrison ("Sawyer's") being established on his land. In King Philip's attack, February tenth, 1675/6, his son Ephraim was killed, either at "Sawyer's" or at "Prescott's," in Clinton. All the Sawyers west of Middlesex County seem to have been descendants of THOMAS[1]. He had eleven children, viz.:

1. THOMAS[2] SAWYER, born 1648 or 1649; married (1), 1670, Sarah ——, (2) 1672, HANNAH LEWIS, (3) 1718, Mary White; died 1736.
2. Ephraim[2] Sawyer, born 1650; killed by Indians in 1675.
3. Marie[2] Sawyer, born 1652.
4. Joshua[2] Sawyer, born 1655; married, 1678, Sarah Potter, of Woburn.
5. James[2] Sawyer, born 1657; married, February fourth, 1687, Mary Marble.
6. Caleb[2] Sawyer, born 1659.
7. John[2] Sawyer, born 1661.
8. Elizabeth[2] Sawyer, born 1663.
9. Deborah[2] Sawyer, born 1666; died in infancy.
10. Nathaniel[2] Sawyer, born 1670.
11. Martha[2] Sawyer, born 1673.

In the Lancaster Cemetery is his grave stone, inscribed as follows:

THOMAS
SAWYER
Dec'd Sep-
tember 12, 1706.

2. THOMAS[2] SAWYER (THOMAS[1]), of Lancaster, Mass., was the first white child born in the town. He

was born on the second or twelfth of May or July, 1648 or 1649. He married (1), August eleventh, 1670, Sarah ———, who died January second, 1672, leaving a child, Mary, born November thirtieth, 1671. On September twenty-first, 1672, he married (2) HANNAH[2] LEWIS (WILLIAM[1]); and (3) July fifteenth, 1718, Mary White, who died August twenty-second, 1733. In 1708, he, his son Elias[3], and John Bigelow were captured and taken to Canada by the Indians. Now the name of Sawyer has ever been associated with mills and mill-saws; accordingly, when the party reached Montreal, THOMAS[2] SAWYER offered to put up a mill on the River Chambly, on condition that the French Governor should obtain a release of all the captives. There was no difficulty in effecting the ransom of Bigelow and young Sawyer; but the Indians were determined that THOMAS[2] SAWYER, who had the reputation of being a very brave man, should be put to death by lingering tortures. Artifice at length secured his release. A friar appeared suddenly, doubtless by arrangement with the Governor, and said that he held the key to Purgatory in his hand, and that if they did not release the prisoner without delay, he would unlock the gate and cast them in headlong. Their superstitious fears being aroused, the Indians unbound SAWYER, who was already tied to the stake, and yielded him to the Governor. He finished the mill, which was the first one built in Canada, before the year was

out, and was sent home in company with Bigelow. Elias³ Sawyer was detained a while, to
teach the Canadians the art of sawing and keep-
ing the mill in order; he was finally dismissed
with rich presents. In the Lancaster Cemetery
is the gravestone of THOMAS², inscribed as follows:

Here lyes Buried
yᵉ Body of Mr
THOMAS SAWYER
Who died September
5th, 1736, in yᵉ 89th
Year of his Age.

THOMAS² SAWYER held many positions of
trust; among others, that of Representative to
the General Court in 1707. His oldest son,
Bezaleel³, died before his father; the next oldest,
who was

3. WILLIAM³ SAWYER (THOMAS²⁻¹), was a child of the
second marriage (with HANNAH LEWIS). He
was born in February, 1679, and in 1700 married
MARY³ HOUGHTON (JOHN²⁻¹). Some say his
first wife was HANNAH³ HOUGHTON; but he left
a widow Mary, at his death, in 1741. He
raised a family of twelve children, as follows:

1. Mary⁴ Sawyer; married Phinehas Willard.
2. Hannah⁴ Sawyer; married John Snow.
3. Hepzibah⁴ Sawyer; married Increase Powers.
4. AHOLIAB⁴ Sawyer; "eldest son," baptized 1711.
5. William⁴ Sawyer; "second son".
6. Josiah⁴ Sawyer; "third son".
7. Thankful⁴ Sawyer; married Jonathan Fairbanks.
8. Benjamin⁴ Sawyer.
9. Dr. Israel⁴ Sawyer.
10. Martha⁴ Sawyer; married Charles Wilder.
11. Joseph⁴ Sawyer.
12. Uriah⁴ Sawyer.

4. AHOLIAB[4] SAWYER, of Lancaster and Bolton, Massachusetts (WILLIAM[3], THOMAS[2-1]), is shown by the administration papers of his father's estate to be the oldest of WILLIAM'S[3] seven sons. Under date of 1741 we read:

Then sett off to Aholiab the eldest son that Peice of Land where he now Dwells Bounded westerly by Gates land, etc.

In the same document William[4] is called the second son, and Josiah the third. Since his father was married in 1700 and Aholiab was baptized in 1711, his birth is bounded by those dates. Though he was the oldest son, he had five sisters, and some of them may have been older than he. In 1735 he married BETTY (or ELIZABETH[4]) SAWYER (EPHRAIM[3], JAMES[2], THOMAS[1]), a distant cousin, for they had the same great-grandfather (see chart). BETTY was born in 1711 and lived past the century mark, dying in 1815. No record of AHOLIAB's death has been found; he was living in 1764. The children of AHOLIAB[4] and BETTY[4] (SAWYER) SAWYER were as follows:

1. Submit[5] Sawyer, born June seventeenth, 1736.
2. Elizabeth[5] Sawyer, born September twenty-fifth, 1737.
3. Mary[5] Sawyer, born September thirtieth, 1738.
4. Aholiab[5] Sawyer, born May twenty-seventh, 1742.
5. Sibillah[5] Sawyer, born March eighth, 1744-5.
6. Elizabeth[5] Sawyer, born May twenty-ninth, 1747. Evidently the first Elizabeth had died young.
7. Ephraim[5] Sawyer, born November twentieth, 1749.
8. Israel[5] Sawyer, born September ninth, 1751.
9. Susannah[5] Sawyer, born February, 1754.
10. GEORGE[5] Sawyer, born November twenty-fifth, 1757 (O. S., or Dec. 6, N. S)

5. GEORGE[5] SAWYER, of Bolton, Massachusetts, and
Stark and Smithfield, Maine (AHOLIAB[4], WIL-
LIAM[3], THOMAS[2-1]), when a little more than
seventeen years of age, is found enrolled in
Captain Artemas How's Militia Company during the "Lexington Alarm" in 1775. Whether
he took part in the battle is uncertain; but
he was evidently one of the Minute Men ready
to report wherever ordered. During the siege
of Boston he was serving under Captain Samuel
Woods, later under Captain Jonathan Houghton, and in the "Jerseys," in 1776-1777, under
Captain David Nurse. Thus far he had served
as a private; but the Military Secretary at
Washington writes us, in reply to our inquiry:

It is shown by the records that GEORGE SAWYER served
as a Sergeant in Capt. Seth Newton's Company of
Stearns's Regiment, Massachusetts Militia, in the Revolutionary War. His name is found on a muster roll of the
company dated May 21, 1778.

In his application for a pension in after years,
we find that in 1780 SERGEANT GEORGE[5] SAW-
YER was serving in 1780, under a Captain Sawyer, and that he took part in the Battle of Har-
lem Heights. His pension claim was allowed.

Leaving the Revolutionary Army in 1780, we
next hear of GEORGE[5] SAWYER as marrying LUCY[6]
MERRITT (NOAH[5], JONATHAN[4], JOHN[3-2], HENRY[1]).
They seem to have left Bolton, Massachusetts.
George's grandson, Henry Sawyer Doyen, of
Cornville, Me., says: "I have heard my mother
[Sarah Lee (Sawyer) Doyen], say something

about their coming from Charlotteville, Ontario, Canada East, to Stark, Maine; that in the time of the Revolutionary War they took the side of the Americans, and that the British persecuted them, and they had to flee that country; and that they then came to Stark and settled there. Looking over the town records of Stark I found that GEORGE[5] SAWYER was one of the men who organized the town in 1794; that he was one of the Board of Selectmen for a number of years; that in 1812 they moved to Smithfield and died there."

They were buried in the Smithfield burying ground. A double stone marks their resting place, with the following inscription:

On one side:

Sergeant
GEORGE SAWYER,
Son of Aholiab Sawyer.
Born in Bolton, Mass., Dec. 6, 1757.
Died in Smithfield, Maine, Apr. 30, 1842.
AE 94.
A Soldier in the Revolutionary War.

On the other side:

LUCY,
Daughter of
Noah Merritt and Sarah Lee,
Wife of
GEORGE SAWYER.
Born in Templeton, Mass., May 25, 1762.
Died in Smithfield, Maine, March 2, 1832.

The children of GEORGE[5] and LUCY[6] (MERRITT) SAWYER were:

1. Henry[6] Sawyer, born December ninth, 1786; died September, 1788.

2. Betsy[6] Sawyer, born February third, 1789; married 1812, Andrew Munsey, as his second wife (see Part I). She died August eighth, 1848.
3. Otis[6] Sawyer, born in East Mercer, April nineteenth, 1792; married 1816, Mahala Leathers; died February twelfth, 1826.
4. Josiah[6] Sawyer, born August twelfth, 1798; married March third, 1823, Sarah Boston; died October twenty-seventh, 1863.
5. Lucy[6] Sawyer, born December twenty-fourth, 1798; married ——— Bailey.
6. Sarah Lee[6] Sawyer, born September twentieth, 1801; married Jeremiah Doyen; died May second, 1866.
7. George[6] Sawyer, born April eighth, 1805; died December fifth, 1857, unmarried.

By the marrriage of Betsey Sawyer, in 1812, the name of Sawyer was merged in that of Munsey.

AUTHORITIES

1. "Sawyers in America," Carter.
2. Nourse's "Lancaster."
3. Nourse's "Annals."
4. "Houghton Genealogy."
5. "Lancaster Records."
6. Willard's "Lancaster."
7. "Templeton Records."

THE SOUTHWORTH FAMILY

1. ₁Edward Southworth, of Leyden, Holland, was born 1590±, and died 1621±. He married May twenty-eighth, 1613, Alice[1] Carpenter, who was born in England in 1590± and died in Plymouth, Massachusetts, March twenty-sixth, 1670 (O. S., April fifth, N. S.). She was the daughter of ₁Alexander Carpenter of Wrington, Somersetshire, England (see Carpenter family); on August fourteenth, 1623, she married GOV-

ERNOR WILLIAM BRADFORD of Plymouth
Colony.

Little is known of ₁Edward Southworth. He
was a silk worker in Leyden, one of the Pilgrim
exiles in Rev. John Robinson's church. He was
there as early as 1611, and a brother Thomas
was a witness of his wedding there in 1613. No
documentary evidence has been found to prove
who was his father, though it seems probable
that it was Thomas Southworth of Samlesbury.
If this is correct, the line runs back unbroken for
fourteen generations to Gilbert de Southworth
in the beginning of the thirteenth century.

1. GENERAL CONSTANT[1] SOUTHWORTH of Duxbury,
son of ₁Edward and ALICE[1] (CARPENTER) SOUTH-
WORTH was the first male of his line to take
passage to America. His MOTHER, a widow
(see CARPENTER family), had come in the *Ann*
to Plymouth, leaving her two sons CONSTANT[1]
and Thomas in Leyden, and soon after had married GOVERNOR BRADFORD.

In 1628, when CONSTANT[1] was about fourteen years old, he rejoined his mother at Plymouth; soon after his brother, two years his
junior, also came. GOVERNOR BRADFORD
proved a kind father, and the boys grew up into
leading citizens. CONSTANT[1] settled in Duxbury, was a volunteer —"though young"—for
the Pequot War of 1637, and the same year
married ELIZABETH[2] COLLIER (WILLIAM[1]) (see
COLLIER family). For seventeen years he was

Deputy from Duxbury, and for sixteen years
Treasurer of the Colony. On the death of his
younger brother he succeeded him as Assistant
and served for nine years. He went to King
Philip's War, though he was past sixty, but soon
yielded his place to his son-in-law, Benjamin
Church, the great Indian fighter. Goodwin
says:

> For several generations those who bore the name of
> Southworth, and those who married the female descend-
> ants, were almost without exception brave soldiers in the
> Colonial Wars. A condensed account of GENERAL CON-
> STANT[1] SOUTHWORTH's military and civil record, taken
> from the Year Book of the Society of Colonial Wars, is
> as follows: GENERAL CONSTANT SOUTHWORTH (1615-1679)
> served in the Pequot War, 1637; ensign Duxbury Com-
> pany, 1646; Lieut. 1653; Deputy from 1647 for twenty-two
> years; Treasurer of Plymouth Colony for sixteen years;
> Member of the Council of War, 1658; Commissioner
> for the United Colonies, 1668. Commissary General
> during King Philip's War; Governor of Kennebec. He
> died March tenth, 1679-80, aged about sixty-five years.

The children of CONSTANT[1] and ELIZABETH[2]
(COLLIER) SOUTHWORTH were:

1. Alice[2]   2. MERCY[2]   3. Priscilla[2]
4. Edward[2]   5. Nathaniel[2]   6. William[2]
7. Mary[2]   8. Elizabeth[2]

2. MERCY[2] SOUTHWORTH (CONSTANT[1]) was born in
   Duxbury about 1638. On May twelfth, 1658,
   she was married at Eastham to SAMUEL[2] FREE-
   MAN of the same town, son of SAMUEL[1] of Watertown (see FREEMAN II family). She died November twenty-fifth, 1712.

By the marriage of MERCY[2] SOUTHWORTH, in 1658,
  the name of SOUTHWORTH was merged in that of FREEMAN II;
  in 1695
  the name of FREEMAN II* was merged in that of PEPPER;
  in 1754
  the name of PEPPER   was merged in that of MEREEN,
  in 1784
  the name of MEREEN   was merged in that of HOPKINS,
  and in 1847
  the name of HOPKINS   was merged in that of **MUNSEY.**

AUTHORITIES

1. "Southworth Genealogy."
2. *Mayflower Descendant*, Vol. 3.
3. Goodwin's "Pilgrim Republic."
4. Savage, "Genealogical Dictionary."
5. Society of Colonial Wars: "Year Book" (1895).

THE SPRAGUE FAMILY

1. FRANCIS[1] SPRAGUE, of Duxbury, Massachusetts, sailed from London for New England in 1623, with Anna and Mercy, his daughters, or possibly his WIFE and daughter. They reached Plymouth in the latter part of June, in the *Ann*. The same year three acres of land were allotted to him "to the sea eastward." In 1627, at the time of the division of cattle, FRANCIS[1] SPRAGUE was in the "sixt lott," of thirteen persons, consisting of the Adamses, WINSLOWS, Bassetts, and Spragues. Besides FRANCIS[1] SPRAGUE, we find Anna and Mercy mentioned, and we may be sure there was no other Sprague in the colony at

---

* The Freemans II also became Munseys by the Hopkins route direct in 1719, when CALEB[4] HOPKINS married MERCY[4] FREEMAN II.

that time. Probably his two children John[2]
and Dorcas[2] were born in Plymouth or in Duxbury.

In 1632, Duxbury was set off from Plymouth,
and in 1637, incorporated as a town. The following year Francis[1] was licensed as an inn-
holder there, and continued there at least until
1666. He is spoken of as being "a man of influence and property." He was one of the
original proprietors of Bridgewater (1645),
though he never resided there. In 1660 he
became one of the purchasers of Dartmouth.

His WIFE's maiden name is unknown, and her
Christian name is in dispute; possibly he married a second wife in America. He had at least
three children, and if Anna was not his WIFE,
but his daughter, he had four. The other three
were:

1. Mercy[2]   2. John[2]   3. Dorcas[2]

The date of his death is not known, but it falls
between 1666 and 1669.

2. John[2] Sprague (Francis[1]) of Duxbury succeeded to his father's business in 1669. His
birthdate has not been found, but it is probable
that he was born in Plymouth. In 1655 he
married Ruth[2] Bassett (William[1]) of Duxbury (see Bassett family). They lived for a
time in Marshfield. John[2] was killed by the
Indians in the fight at Pawtucket, March twenty-
sixth, 1676. His WIDOW later married ——

Thomas. The children of JOHN[2] and RUTH[2] (BASSETT) SPRAGUE were:—

1. John[3]   2. WILLIAM[3]   3. Ruth[3]
4. Elizabeth[3]   5. Desire[3]   6. Samuel[3]
7. Dorcas[3]

3. WILLIAM[3] SPRAGUE (JOHN[2], FRANCIS[1]) of Duxbury married, at some unknown date, GRACE[3] WADSWORTH (DEACON JOHN[2], CHRISTOPHER[1]), also of Duxbury (see WADSWORTH family). He was chosen "Surveyor of Highways" March seventeenth, 1708. He was drowned November twenty-fifth, 1712, by the upsetting of a whale boat. His WIDOW married Josiah Wormall of Duxbury, December twenty-fifth, 1723. She died in 1758.

The children of WILLIAM[3] and GRACE[3] (WADSWORTH) SPRAGUE, all born in Duxbury, were:—

1. Ruth[4]   2. Zeruiah[4]   3. JETHRO[4]   4. Terah[4]

4. JETHRO[4] SPRAGUE (WILLIAM[3], JOHN[2], FRANCIS[1]) of Duxbury, Massachusetts, and Cape Small Point, Maine, was born in Duxbury, November thirtieth, 1709. He married (1), December twelfth, 1738 PATIENCE[5] BARTLETT (JOSEPH[4], SAMUEL[3], BENJAMIN[2], ROBERT[1]), a descendant of *eight Mayflower* Pilgrims (see BARTLETT family). He married (2) Mrs. Bethiah (Sprague) Cushing, daughter of Samuel[3] Sprague (Samuel[2], William[1]) of Duxbury, a descendant of William[1] of Hingham.

JETHRO[4] SPRAGUE was one of the enterprising citizens of Duxbury; he owned a farm and a country store; built schooners; and had a public house, called "Sprague's Tavern." He was chosen constable March twentieth, 1748, but declined to serve. He was on the petit and grand juries at Plymouth Court in 1760. In 1761, in a small craft of his own building, he took his family and sailed for Maine. He settled at Cape Small Point, in Georgetown (now Phippsburg), and engaged in lumbering, fishing, and tailoring. He bought and lived in Bliffin's (or Blethen's) farm. The last record of him is in 1773, when he conveys land in Duxbury to his sister, Zeruiah, (Sprague) Chandler.

The children of Jethro[4] and Patience[5] (Bartlett) Sprague so far as known were:—

1. Sylvanus[6] or Silvina   2. William[5]

5. Lieutenant William[5] Sprague (Jethro[4], William[3], John[2], Francis[1]), of Phippsburg, Maine, was a tailor, farmer, and soldier. He was born May or November nineteenth, 1740, and died March twenty-fifth, 1829. He married March second, 1763, Mrs. Miriam[5] (Day) Blethen, widow of James Blethen, whom she had married July thirtieth, 1757. She died October fifth, 1836 (see Day family).

In 1776 William[5] Sprague was commissioned as 1st Lieutenant in Captain James Cobb, Jr.'s (Fourth) Company, First Lincoln County Regiment of Massachusetts Militia. He was a Revolutionary pensioner, and was at times called "Captain," although the reason is not obvious. It was probably a kind of honorary title.

The children of WILLIAM[5] and MIRIAM[5] (DAY) Blethen-SPRAGUE, all born in Phippsburg, were:—

1. William[6]	2. Jethro[6]	3. Nelson[6]
4. Grace[6]	5. Patience[6]	6. Sylvina[6]
7. Mary[6]	8. Lovina[6]	

6. WILLIAM[6] SPRAGUE (LIEUTENANT WILLIAM[5], JETHRO[4], WILLIAM[3], JOHN[2], FRANCIS[1]), of Georgetown (Phippsburg), Maine, was born in May, 1767. On December seventeenth, 1789, he was married by Rev. Ezekiel Emerson to RACHEL[3] McINTYRE (JOSEPH[2], WILLIAM[1]) of Georgetown. She was born in 1772, and died August twenty-fifth, 1841. He was a farmer and millwright; he also served in the War of 1812. He died October fifth, 1848, aged eighty-one years, five months. His wife died August twenty-fifth, 1841. They were buried at Small Point, on his farm.

The children of WILLIAM[6] and RACHEL[3] (McINTYRE) SPRAGUE were eleven in number:

1. Sally[7]	2. Thankful[7]	3. Polly[7]
4. Nathaniel[7]	5. Thomas Hardy[7]	6. Alden[7]
7. Alfred[7]	8. Miriam[7]	9. Charlotte[7]
10. Caroline[7]	11. Rachel[7]	

7. MIRIAM[7] SPRAGUE (WILLIAM[6], LIEUTENANT WILLIAM[5], JETHRO[4], WILLIAM[3], JOHN[2], FRANCIS[1]), of Small Point, Phippsburg, was born March sixteenth, 1792; on August thirteenth, 1812, she married ELISHA[7] HOPKINS (ELISHA[6], SIMEON[5], CALEB[4-3], GILES[2], STEPHEN[1]) of Harpswell (see HOPKINS LINE). She died January twentieth, 1876.

By the marriage of MIRIAM[7] SPRAGUE, in 1812,
    the name of SPRAGUE   was merged in that of HOPKINS,
and in 1847
    the name of HOPKINS was merged in that of MUNSEY.

AUTHORITIES

1. *Mayflower Descendant*, Vol. 2.
2. Winsor's "Duxbury."
3. "Sprague Families in America."
4. Austin's "Genealogical Dictionary."
5. *N. E. Historical and Genealogical Register*, Vol. 3.
6. Savage's "Genealogical Dictionary."
7. Goodwin's "Pilgrim Republic."
8. "Sprague Memorial."
9. Daggett's "Attleboro."
10. Duxbury "Vital Records."
11. "Probate Records, Plymouth County."
12. "Wadsworth Family."
13. "Massachusetts Soldiers and Sailors of the Revolutionary War."
14. *Maine Historical Society Collections*, 2d series (1899), X. 322.
15. Affidavit of Marcellus D. Sprague (M. G. I. 157; III. 135).

THE STOCKBRIDGE FAMILY

1. JOHN[1] STOCKBRIDGE, a wheelwright by trade, came to New England in the *Blessing*, John Leicester, master, in June, 1635. He was then twenty-seven years old; therefore he was born in 1608. His wife, ANNE, was twenty-one and their son Charles a year old. He went to Scituate, where, in 1638, he took the oath of fidelity. His wife died about 1642, and he married (2) Mrs. Elizabeth (Hatch) Soan in 1643. His third wife was Mary ——, who survived him. He was one of the Conihasset partners in 1646.

He owned a large tract of land near "Stockbridge's Mill pond." In 1656 he purchased one-half a mill privilege of George Russell, together with a saw mill which Isaac Stedman had erected ten years before. He then built a grist mill, in partnership with Mr. Russell. The same year, probably, he built the Stockbridge Mansion House, which was a garrison in King Philip's War. When the building was torn down—in 1840—bullets were found imbedded in the timbers, which the Indians had fired at the inmates during a siege.

JOHN[1] STOCKBRIDGE died August thirteenth, 1657. His children were as follows:

By the first wife, ANNE:

1. Charles[2]   2. Hannah[2]   3. ELIZABETH[2]

By the second wife, Elizabeth (Hatch) Soan:

4. Sarah[2]   5. Hester[2]

By the third wife, who later m. Daniel Henrick:

6. Abigail[2]   7. John[2] (probably died young)

(Since the Ancestral Chart was made, it has been found that ANNE was the mother of ELIZABETH[2], who was born in 1639).

2. ELIZABETH[2] STOCKBRIDGE (JOHN[1]) was born in Scituate in 1639/40. Her mother was the first wife of JOHN[1]. She married in 1661 THOMAS[2] HYLAND (see HYLAND family).

By the marriage of ELIZABETH[2] STOCKBRIDGE, in 1661,
    the name of STOCKBRIDGE was merged in that of HYLAND; in 1686
    the name of HYLAND   was merged in that of MERRITT; in 1786
    the name of MERRITT   was merged in that of SAWYER; in 1812
    the name of SAWYER   was merged in that of MUNSEY.

AUTHORITIES

1. "American Ancestry," Vol. 3.
2. Barry's "Sketch of Hanover, Massachusetts."
3. Deane's "Scituate."
4. Savage's "Genealogical Dictionary."
5. *N. E. Historical and Genealogical Register*, Vols. 70, 71.
6. "Ninth Report, Record Commissioners, Boston," Births.

THE TREAT FAMILY

1. Richard[1] Treat (1Robert, 2Richard, 3William, 4John) was born in 1584, in Pitminster, Somerset, England. He married April twenty-seventh 1615, in Pitminster, Alice Gaylord, daughter of Hugh. Richard[1] was one of the first settlers of Wethersfield, Connecticut, where we find him chosen juror on June fifteenth, 1643. This was "a high position then, generally occupied only by the most prominent persons." He was also called "Mr.",—"a title fully as high as *Honorable* is now."* In 1644 he was chosen Deputy. and annually elected as such for fourteen years, After this he was eight times elected Assistant. "He must have been a man of high social standing and of much influence in the town." When the General Court secured a charter for the Connecticut Colony in 1662, Richard[1] Treat and two of his sons-in-law were among the nineteen patentees, or charter members, to whom Charles II sent the famous document. Richard[1] was a man of considerable wealth, and an extensive land owner. His farms consisted of from

---

* See footnote, page 27, and Index of Subjects.

one thousand to one thousand five hundred acres. He died some time between October eleventh, 1669, and March third, 1690/70. His widow survived him. Their children were:—

1. Honor[2]	2. Joanna[2]	3. Sarah[2]
4. Richard[2]	5. Robert[2]	6. Elizabeth[2]
7. Susanna[2]	8. Alice[2]	9. James[2]
10. Katherine[2]		

2. Governor Robert[2] Treat (Richard[1]), of Milford, Connecticut, was born in 1624±, in Pitminster, Somerset, England. He came with his father to America, but seems to have left Wethersfield, Connecticut, where his father settled, at an early age; for in 1639, we find him in Milford. Though at that time he was less than sixteen years old, he was one of the nine appointed to survey and lay out the lands of the new town, just purchased of the Indians. Sometime previous to 1648 he married (1) Jane[2], daughter of Edward[1] (or Edmund) Tapp. She died in 1703, and he married (2), at the age of eighty-one, Mrs. Elizabeth (Powell) [Hollingsworth-Bryan], a lady of only sixty-four; yet he survived her several years, dying July twelfth, 1710.

Robert[2] Treat was the eighth Governor of Connecticut. He was Lieutenant-Governor from 1676-82, then Governor from 1683-87. On the thirty-first day of October, in 1687, Sir Edmund Andros usurped the government and demanded the Charter of the Colony, which Richard[1] Treat, the Governor's father, had

helped to secure from Charles II. GOVERNOR
TREAT sent for it, and told the Secretary to put
it in the box where it had lain and leave the key
in the box. He feared that if the charter were
surrendered, the Colony would get a far less
liberal one, or perhaps none at all. So he had
the debate prolonged until candle lighting;
then, at a preconcerted signal, the lights were
extinguished, and a Captain Wadsworth, in the
confusion, carried off the charter. He secreted
it in a hollow of the famous Charter Oak, in
Hartford, where it lay until a change of government occurred in England. When William and
Mary came to the throne, Sir Edmund Andros
found himself in disfavor, and finally was im-
prisoned in Boston. On May ninth, 1689, at the
urgent request of the people, GOVERNOR TREAT
and his magistrates resumed the government of
the Colony. They took the charter from its
hiding place and continued as before. GOVER-
NOR TREAT held his high office until 1697. He
had been Lieutenant-Governor, as we have said,
from 1676-82, and from 1698-1707 was again
Lieutenant-Governor. Thus with the exception of Andros's brief usurpation, ROBERT²
TREAT served the Colony continuously, as Lieutenant-Governor or Governor, from 1676 to
1707, or thirty-two years.

In Frederick C. Norton's "Governors of Connecticut," after reading of the "priceless services
of ROBERT² TREAT, rendered to the Colony during a critical period," we find this tribute to his
military skill, quoted from Hollister:

> GOVERNOR TREAT was not only a man of high courage,
> but was one of the most cautious military leaders,
> and possessed a quick sagacity, united with a
> breadth of understanding that enabled him to see
> at a glance the most complex relations that sur-
> rounded the field of battle.

This refers to the fact, less generally known, that he was Commander at the "Great Swamp Fight"; Major commanding the Connecticut troops at the battles of Hadley and Springfield; and that in the encounter with the Indians at Bloody Brook, September eighteenth, 1675, his arrival on the scene with the Connecticut forces turned the tide. Indeed, it was his military prowess that brought him political preferment, and enabled him to show that he was a statesman as well as a soldier. He died, full of years, July twelfth, 1710.

The following were the children of GOVERNOR ROBERT[2] and JANE[2] (TAPP) TREAT of whom record has been found, though tradition asserts that they had twenty-one!

1. SAMUEL[3]	2. John[3]	3. Mary[3]
4. Robert[3]	5. Sarah[3]	6. Abigail[3]
7. Hannah[3]	8. Joseph[3]	

3. REV. SAMUEL[3] TREAT (GOVERNOR ROBERT[2], RICHARD[1]), of Eastham, Massachusetts, was baptized September third, 1648, in Milford, Connecticut, shortly after his birth. He was graduated from Harvard College in 1669. He studied for the ministry, and in 1672 was called to Nauset (Eastham), as a successor of REV. JOHN[1] MAYO, at a salary of fifty pounds per annum. Later his salary was increased, and he

received a considerable gift of land. He married (1), March sixteenth, 1674, ELIZABETH[3] MAYO (CAPTAIN SAMUEL[2], REV. JOHN[1]), of Barnstable. She died December fourth, 1696, and MR. TREAT married (2), August twenty-ninth, 1700, Mrs. Abigail (Willard) Estabrook, daughter of President Willard, of Harvard College. REV. MR. TREAT was greatly beloved by his people, and the Indians revered him as a father. When he died, March eighteenth, 1716/7, they begged the privilege of helping to bear his body to the grave. His tombstone, still in good condition, may be seen at Eastham. His children were:

By ELIZABETH[3] MAYO:

1. JANE[4]	2. Elizabeth[4]	3. Sarah[4]
4. Samuel[4]	5. Mary[4]	6. Robert[4]
7. Abigail[4]	8. Joseph[4]	9. Joshua[4]
10. John[4]	11. Nathaniel[4]	

By Abigail (Willard) Estabrook:

1. Eunice[4]	2. Robert 2d[4]

REV. SAMUEL[3] TREAT was the grandfather of Robert Treat Paine, one of the Signers of the Declaration of Independence, by his daughter, Eunice[4], who married Rev. Thomas Paine.

4. JANE[4] TREAT (REVEREND SAMUEL[3], GOVERNOR ROBERT[2], RICHARD[1]) was born in Eastham, December sixth, 1675. On the eleventh day of October, 1694, she married CONSTANT[3] FREE-

MAN (SAMUEL², SAMUEL¹), of Truro (see FREE-
MAN II family).

By the marriage of JANE⁴ TREAT, in 1694,
  the name of TREAT   was merged in that of FREEMAN II;
  in 1719
  the name of FREEMAN II was merged in that of HOPKINS,
  and in 1847
  the name of HOPKINS was merged in that of **MUNSEY.**

AUTHORITIES

1. "The Treat Genealogy."
2. Hinman's "Letters from Kings and Queens."
3. Society of Colonial Wars: "Illinois, 1900."
4. Norton's "Governors of Connecticut."
5. "Freeman Genealogy."
6. Freeman's "Cape Cod."
7. Goodwin's "Genealogical Notes."
8. Sibley's "Harvard Graduates," Vol. 2.

THE WADSWORTH FAMILY

The Wadsworths of America maintain that
the family came originally from Normandy,
settled in Kent, and had a coat of arms dating
from the battle of Crécy, in 1346. This coat of
arms is: a shield *gules*, three *fleurs de lis*, stalked
and slipped, *argent;* the crest: on a terrestrial
globe wingéd ppr. an eagle rising *or;* the motto:
Aquila non captat muscas. In plain language
this means: Three white lilies on a red shield,
surmounted by a winged globe supporting a
yellow eagle. The Latin motto signifies: "An
eagle does not catch flies."

1. CHRISTOPHER¹ WADSWORTH came to America in
   1632 on the ship *Lion.* He settled, lived, and

died at Duxbury. It is not known whether he
was married when he came, for he was then
young. His wife's first name was GRACE. Some
maintain that her family name was Cole, but
that remains uncertain. MR. WADSWORTH
quickly entered into the life of the community
and was elected to positions of honor and trust.
Within two years of his arrival he was chosen to
the highest office in the town,—constable, or
high sheriff. Three times he was sent as a
Deputy to the General Court. Winsor, in his
"History of Duxbury," gives him high praise.
Speaking of CHRISTOPHER[1]'s descendants, he
says:

> No family of the town presents a greater array of learned
> men, men who have been distinguished in the civil
> and religious government of their native town, who
> have held a high rank in the literary institutions of
> New England, and whose names stand with honor
> on the muster rolls of the Revolution.

He died in 1675. His children were:—

1. Capt. Samuel[2]   2. Joseph[2]   3. JOHN[2]   4. Mary

2. DEACON JOHN[2] WADSWORTH (CHRISTOPHER[1])
was born in Duxbury in 1638. He lived and
died on the homestead. For many years he was
a deacon of the church. Four times he was sent
as a Deputy to the General Court. In 1667 he
married ABIGAIL[2] ANDREWS (HENRY[1]) of Taunton (see ANDREWS family). He died May fifteenth, 1700, "about sixty-two yeares of age."
His children were:

1. Mary[3]	2. Abigail[3]	3. John[3]
4. Christopher[3]	5. Ichabod[3]	6. Isaac[3]
7. Lydia[3]	8. Sarah[3]	9. GRACE[2]
10. Hopestill[3]	11. Mercy[3]	12. Hannah[3]

Through his son John[3] Wadsworth he was the lineal ancestor of the poet Longfellow, as follows:—

John[3] married Mercy Wiswell, their son,
Peleg[4], married Susannah Sampson, their son,
Gen. Peleg[5], married Elizabeth Bartlett; their daughter,
Zilpha[6], married Stephen Longfellow; their son was
Henry Wadsworth Longfellow.

3. GRACE[3] WADSWORTH (DEACON JOHN[2], CHRISTOPHER[1]) was born before 1680. Before February twenty-second, 1701/2, she married WILLIAM[3] SPRAGUE (JOHN[2], FRANCIS[1]) of Duxbury (see SPRAGUE family). She outlived her husband, who was drowned. She made her father her executor, and died before June eighteenth, 1688.

By the marriage of GRACE[3] WADSWORTH, before 1701/2,
the name of WADSWORTH was merged in that of SPRAGUE;
in 1812
the name of SPRAGUE was merged in that of HOPKINS;
and in 1847
the name of HOPKINS was merged in that of **MUNSEY.**

AUTHORITIES

1. "The Wadsworth Genealogy."
   "Two Hundred and Fifty Years of the Wadsworth Family in America."
2. "Lawrence and Bartlett Memorials."
3. Winsor's "Duxbury."
4. "Sprague Families in America."
5. *Genealogical Advertiser*, Vol. 1.
6. *Mayflower Descendant*, Vol. 9.

THE WARREN FAMILY

1. RICHARD[1] WARREN was one of those who joined the *Mayflower* in England, and was one of the "principal men" of the company. His two sons followed in 1621, and his wife ELIZABETH and five daughters came over in the *Ann* or the *Little James*. It has been stated, as confidently as if it were known to be true, that RICHARD[1] was the son of Christopher Warren and Alice Webb, daughter of Thomas Webb of Sidnam, Devonshire, England; and that he married Mrs. Elizabeth (Jouatt) Marsh. But the last statement has been *proved* impossible (*Mayflower Descendant*, 2:63), and the first is very uncertain. Nothing is actually known of his parentage, or of the maiden name of his wife. We merely know that her first name was ELIZABETH (*Mayflower Descendant*, 1:152).

RICHARD[1] WARREN was the twelfth signer of the *Mayflower* Compact. He was one of the earliest of the Colonial warriors, for he served under CAPTAIN MILES STANDISH in the first encounter at Great Meadow, Wellfleet Harbor, on December eighth, 1620 (O. S.), three days before the landing at Plymouth. He lived long enough to beget two sons in America, but died in 1628. Secretary Morton, who knew him well, said: "He was a useful instrument, and during his life bore a deep share in the difficulties and troubles of this first settlement." His wife survived him, and the records show that from time to time she gave lands to the husbands of her daughters.

The children of RICHARD[1] and ELIZABETH WARREN were born in England, with the exception of the last two:—

1. MARY[2] WARREN married, in 1628, ROBERT BARTLETT
2. Anna[2] Warren, married, April nineteenth, 1633, Thomas Little.
3. Sarah[2] Warren, married, in 1634, John Cooke.
4. Elizabeth[2] Warren, married, in 1636, Richard Church, and was mother of the famous Indian fighter, Benjamin Church.
5. Abigail[2] Warren, married, in 1639, Anthony Snow
6. Nathaniel[2] Warren, born in Plymouth in 1624; married, in 1645, Sarah Walker.
7. Joseph[2] Warren, born in Plymouth; married Priscilla Faunce.

MARY[2] WARREN (RICHARD[1]) was born in England. She, with her mother and sisters, were "Pilgrims," but not *Mayflower* passengers. In 1628 she married ROBERT[1] BARTLETT, of Plymouth, who had been her fellow passenger in the *Ann* (see BARTLETT family).

By the marriage of MARY[2] WARREN, in 1628,
  the name of WARREN was merged in that of BARTLETT;
  in 1738
  the name of BARTLETT was merged in that of SPRAGUE;
  in 1812
  the name of SPRAGUE was merged in that of HOPKINS;
  and in 1847
  the name of HOPKINS was merged in that of **MUNSEY**.

AUTHORITIES

1. *Mayflower Descendant*, Vols. 1, 2, 3, 4.
2. *Boston Transcript*, 1888, 1891, 1895, 1896, 1911.
3. Davis's "Landmarks of Plymouth."
4. Goodwin's "Pilgrim Republic."

5. "Plymouth Court Records," Vol. 1.
6. Bradford's "History of Plymouth Plantation."
7. Society of Colonial Wars: "Illinois 1900."
8. Society of Colonial Wars: "Yearbook" (1897-8).
9. Savage's "Genealogical Dictionary."
10. Hotten's "List of *Mayflower* Passengers."

THE WOODWORTH FAMILY

Originally the name of the Woodworth family was *Woodward*. Indeed, the American pioneer WALTER[1] is called WOODWARD throughout his will, and so affixes his signature thereto. But his son, Benjamin[2], in an oath of inventory on the estate, March second, 1685/6, spelled the name WOODWORTH. Part of his descendants kept one form and part the other. The original name is derived from the forest-keepers, the Wood Wards of the Hundred Rolls in the reign of Edward I.

1. WALTER[1] WOODWORTH came from Kent County, England, to Scituate, Massachusetts, in 1635. He became a rather extensive land owner. He was assigned the third lot on Kent Street, which runs along the ocean front, at the corner of Meeting House Lane, and there he built a house. In that year he owned other land, a tract on the First Herring Brook, not far below Stockbridge Mill, where afterwards stood the residence of the poet Samuel Woodworth (author of "The Old Oaken Bucket," and a lineal descendant through Walter's son, Benjamin[2]). He owned another tract on Walnut Tree Hill, west of the present

Greenbush or South Scituate Railroad Station, in early times called Walter Woodworth's Hill. In 1666 he also purchased sixty acres in Weymouth. He was made a freeman March second, 1644. On June fourth, 1645, he was appointed surveyor of the highways of Scituate, reappointed in 1646, and again appointed in 1656. His name appears frequently in the town records of Scituate as a juror, etc. In 1654 he was a member of the First Church, which ordained Charles Chauncy as their minister. His will, dated November twenty-sixth, 1685, is in the Plymouth County Probate records. He died 1685/6. The name of his wife is unknown.

The children of WALTER[1] WOODWORTH were as follows:

1. Thomas[2]	2. Sarah[2]	3. Benjamin[2]
4. Elizabeth[2]	5. Joseph[2]	6. Mary[2]
7. MARTHA[2]	8. Isaac[2]	9. Mehitable[2]
10. Abigail[2]		

2. MARTHA[2] WOODWORTH (WALTER[1]) of Scituate was bequeathed ten pounds of money and nearly ten acres of land by her father's will. Her five sisters also had a bequest of ten pounds each, but no land. For some reason MARTHA was favored beyond the other daughters. In June, 1679, she married LIEUTENANT ZACHARY[2] DAMON (JOHN[1]), of the same town (see DAMON family).

By the marriage of MARTHA[2] WOODWORTH, in 1679,
the name of WOODWORTH was merged in that of DAMON; in 1727
the name of DAMON was merged in that of MERRITT; in 1786
the name of MERRITT was merged in that of SAWYER; in 1812
the name of SAWYER was merged in that of MUNSEY.

AUTHORITIES

1. *Mayflower Descendant,* Vol. II.
2. *N. E. Historical and Genealogical Register,* Vol. 18.
3. "The Woodworth Genealogy."
4. "The Woodworth Family."
5. "The Woodward Family MS." (in Historic-Genealogical Library).
6. Deane's "Scituate" (which, however, has many errors).

THE WYBORNE FAMILY

The ancestors of THOMAS[1] WYBORNE (WEY-BURN, WYBORN, WIBORN, WIBORNE) have been traced back to ₄*Thomas* of Shoreham, England (1532), ₃*Richard* of Shoreham, ₂*Richard* of Wrotham, Kent, ₁*Richard* of Wrotham, the father of:

1. THOMAS[1] WYBORNE, of Wrotham, England, and Plymouth, Boston, and Scituate, Massachusetts. THOMAS[1] was the seventh and youngest child of ₁*Richard* of Wrotham. He was baptized June fifth, 1580. On the twenty-seventh of November, 1605, he married (1) Emma Millow. Apparently he married (2) ELIZABETH —— in Tenterden, where he seems to have settled as a "saddler" for a short time before leaving for America. In 1638 he came to this country. For a time he remained at Plymouth; but in 1643 he is in the list of those "able to bear arms" at Scituate, where he is also living four years later. In 1648, however, he bought a house on High Street, Boston. In the city he appears to have been rather prominent. He was Commissioner of the Highways and Constable, meanwhile pursuing his trade of saddler. He had

money to loan, invested in some real property, and at his death in 1656, left an estate valued at nearly four hundred pounds. His wife, ELIZABETH, married (2) Henry Felch, being Felch's second wife.

The children of THOMAS[1] and ELIZABETH WYBORNE were:

1. Thomas[2]   2. ELIZABETH[2]   3. James[2]
4. John[2]   5. Mary[2]   6. Jonathan[2]
7. Nathaniel[2]

2. ELIZABETH[2] WYBORNE was born in 1637±. On the second of March, 1655, while living in Boston, she was married "by Captain Atherton of Cambridge" to JOHN[2] MERRITT (HENRY[1]), of Scituate (see MERRITT family).

By the marriage of ELIZABETH[2] WYBORNE, in 1655,
   the name of WYBORNE was merged in that of MERRITT; in 1786
   the name of MERRITT was merged in that of SAWYER; in 1812
   the name of SAWYER was merged in that of MUNSEY.

AUTHORITIES

1. "Weyburn-Wyborn Genealogy."
2. "Ninth Report of Boston Record Commissioners."
3. *N. E. Historical and Genealogical Register*, Vols. (late numbers; articles by Miss French).

INDEX OF PERSONS

185

BACON, Martha (Howland) [Damon], 90
  Peter, 90
BAILEY, Lucy (Sawyer), 160
  ——, 160
BAKER, Delia Mary (Munsey), 44
  Win., 44
BANGS, Apphia, 59
  Bethia, 59
  Edward, 57, 58, 59, 110
  Hannah, 59
  Hannah (Scudder), 58
  Hannah (Smalley), 58
  John, 57, 58
  Jonathan, 58
  Joshua, 58
  Lydia, 58, 59, 110
  Lydia (Hicks), 57, 58
  Mary (Mayo), 58
  Mercy, 59
  Rebecca, 58
  Rebecca (——), 57, 58
  Ruth (——) [Young], 58
  Sarah, 58
  Sarah (——), 58
BANGS family, 57, 110
BARNABY, James, 61
  Lydia (Bartlett), 61
BARNES, Sarah, 62
BARON DE MOUNSEY, 6
BARSTOW, Sarah, 86
BARTLETT } Bathsheba, 63
BARTLIT }
  Benjamin, 60, 61, 62, 63, 79, 140, 165
  Cecilia (——), 60, 61
  Desire (Arnold), 62
  Ebenezer, 62
  Elizabeth, 60, 61, 177
  Elizabeth (Waterman), 62
  Hannah, 62, 63
  Hannah (Paybody), 62
  Hannah (——), 62
  Ichabod, 62
  Isaiah, 63
  John, 62
  Joseph, 60, 62, 63, 165
  Judah, 62
  Lydia, 61, 63
  Lydia (Nelson), 62, 63
  Mary, 19, 60
  Mary (Warren), 59, 60, 61, 179
  Mercy, 61
  Patience, 63, 165, 166
  Priscilla, 60, 79

BARTLETT—*Continued*
  Rebecca, 60, 62
  Robert, 43, 59, 60, 61, 62, 63, 79, 140, 165, 179
  Ruth (Paybody), 62
  Samuel, 60, 62, 63, 140, 165
  Sarah, 60, 62, 63
  Sarah (Barnes), 62
  Sarah (Bartlett), 62
  Sarah (Brewster), 60, 61, 79
  Sarah (Foster), 62
  Susanna (Jenney), 60, 61
  Susanna (Spooner), 62
  William, 62
BARTLETT family, 59, 79, 140, 165, 179
BASS, John, 55
  Ruth (Alden), 55
BASSETT, Abbott, 65
  Cecilia (Leight), 65
  Dorcas (Joyce), 67
  Elizabeth, 64, 66, 67
  Elizabeth (——), 64, 65
  Jane, 67
  Joseph, 67
  Margaret (Oldham), 65
  Martha (Hobart), 67
  Mary (Burt), 66
  Mary (Joyce), 67
  Mary (——), 64, 65
  Nathaniel, 67
  Richard, 66
  Ruth, 67, 164, 165
  Sarah, 67
  William, 64, 65, 66, 67, 164
BASSETT family, 64
BASSETTS, 163
BATE(s), Abigail, 70
  Abigail (Joy), 70
  Andrew, 68
  Ann(e) (——), 67, 68
  Bathsheba, 70
  Benjamin, 67, 69
  Caleb, 70
  Clement 67, 68, 69, 70, 86
  Eleanor, 70
  Elizabeth (Webster), 70
  Esther, 70, 71, 85
  Esther (Hilliard), 69, 70, 86
  Grace (Lincoln), 70
  Hannah, 70
  Hannah (Litchfield), 70
  Henry, 68
  Hopestill, 69
  James, 67, 68, 69

INDEX OF PLACES

203

INDEX OF SUBJECTS

THE END

www.ingramcontent.com/pod-product-compliance
Lightning Source LLC
LaVergne TN
LVHW012203040326
832903LV00003B/98